The Essential B[uyer's Guide]

SUNBE[AM]

ALPINE

All models 1959 to 1968

Your marque expert:
Chris Barker

VELOCE PUBLISHING

THE PUBLISHER OF FINE AUTOMOTIVE BOOKS

Essential Buyer's Guide Series

For post publication news, updates and amendments relating to this book please visit www.veloce.co.uk/books/V4925

BATTLE CRY!   Hubble & Hattie

www.veloce.co.uk

First published in July 2016 by Veloce Publishing Limited, Veloce House, Parkway Farm Business Park, Middle Farm Way, Poundbury, Dorchester DT1 3AR, England. Fax 01305 268864 / e-mail info@veloce.co.uk / web www.veloce.co.uk or www.velocebooks.com. ISBN: 978-1-845849-25-2. UPC: 6-36847-04925-6.

Introduction
– the purpose of this book

The Sunbeam Alpine was produced for only nine years; it was born as the UK finally began to recover from postwar austerity, it thrived in the 'Swinging Sixties,' and it was snuffed out by Chrysler's takeover of the ailing Rootes Group, along with the subsequent plunge down-market and the appearance of new costly regulatory requirements. 69,000 cars were made in total, and the majority were exported.

When the Alpine appeared, it didn't conform to the prevailing expectation that a sports car should be noisy, rough and uncomfortable, but hindsight shows that it was ahead of its time. Now it can be enjoyed because it still looks great, and a good example is both practical and satisfying.

In more than 40 years of Alpine ownership, I have seen (and suffered) the Sunbeam Alpine's evolution from used car to worthless banger, and back to desirable classic. The owners have evolved too, from discerning middle-class buyers, through young tearaways, impecunious enthusiasts, people having a mid-life crisis, and then retired hobbyists and 'investors.' These people mostly had to discover the joys and woes of buying and running an Alpine for themselves – though with help and encouragement from the Sunbeam Alpine Owners' Club and clubs in the USA and elsewhere.

Now there is another generation of younger enthusiasts who want, and can afford, a good example of this well-engineered and stylish car. This book is really for them, although existing owners should find useful information here as well. Writing it has brought home to me the complexities of the five different 'Series' produced in those nine years. Before you actually buy an Alpine, you need to understand the

Alpine evolution. There are many differences between this early Series II and the late Series V. Both are shown here with their hardtops.

differences, and decide what it is you really want. This book will help you; with it you can manage your hunt for the ideal example.

Alpine 'Series'

To follow this book you need to know that when Rootes introduced an update or face-lift, they gave the car a new 'Series' number. This book follows the manufacturer's practice in using Roman numerals for Series I, II, IV and V, but an Arabic 3. See Chapter 17 for a summary of the many differences.

Thanks

My sincere thanks go to the many owners I have met – in pub car parks, at meetings and 'on line' – and who have shared their experiences with me over a period of 40 years. I also want to thank the current Sunbeam Alpine Owners' Club Committee for supporting the writing of this book, and for providing specific advice on relative values and other details. I especially need to thank Andy Goldsmith and my wife Val for reading and commenting on my text, and owners Dave and Louise Holcombe, Andy, Tom and William Goldsmith, Tim Raymond, Bob Standing, Paul Baker and Glenn Brackenridge for assistance with photographs. Individuals providing photographs are credited in the relevant captions, all other photographs are the property of the author.

A note about the Sunbeam Talbot Alpine and Sunbeam Tiger

The first Sunbeam Alpine was a two-seater version of the older Sunbeam-Talbot 90, produced in small numbers in the 1950s, which was a completely different car and is not covered by this book.

The Sunbeam Tiger was made from 1964 to 1967 in parallel with the Alpine Series IV and V. Trimmed Alpine shells were delivered to Jensen, who modified the transmission tunnel and bulkhead, and then assembled the cars. The Tiger had an American Ford V8 of 260 or 289in^3 (4261 or 4737cc), a Ford gearbox and a Salisbury differential. The rear axle had a Panhard rod. The Alpine's steering system was replaced by a rack and pinion which had to be mounted ahead of the front axle, with consequent poor geometry and turning circle. The battery was moved to the boot to make room for the second exhaust. The engine came with an American generator, and the cooling system was different. Other systems and fittings were Alpine. Parts of this book covering body, body fittings, trim, suspension and brakes are therefore relevant to the Tiger. The book does not address aspects which are unique to the Tiger, nor costs and values – except to note that they are much higher than for the Alpine.

Contents

The Essential Buyer's Guide™ currency
At the time of publication a BG unit of currency "●" equals approximately
£1.00/US$1.44/Euro 1.27. Please adjust to suit current exchange rates.

The Alpine is a well-designed sports tourer, at its best on winding A and B roads, and excellent for long distance touring. It's necessary to ask *which* Alpine is right for you. In its nine years of production there were five different 'Series' of Alpines. There was one significant visible change; the other updates were mostly under the skin. The tables in Chapter 17 show the history of the car, and the changes that were made. You may prefer the purity of the original finned Series I, or the performance and practicality of the final Series V.

Tall & short drivers
The later cars – Series 3-V – have more adjustments, and are better for taller drivers' legs, but the earlier models are adequate.

Controls
The controls are well laid out and mostly pleasant to use, except that the un-assisted brakes of the Series I-II are rather heavy. Steering is also heavy when parking, but fine on the move. The handbrake is next to the driver's door, so you can simultaneously engage first gear and release the brake. The Series IV-V indicator stalk is on the right (RHD), and the headlamp dipswitch is operated by the left foot. Overdrive is operated by a column stalk, opposite the indicators. These are logical, but different to most modern cars.

The early finned Alpine with steel wheels and the optional aluminium hardtop in black. This Series II is almost identical to the Series I, except for the full-height door front chrome pillar.

The last Series V with non-standard alloy wheels and coachline, and the later, more angular GT steel hardtop. None of the parts above the waistline is interchangeable with the Series I and II.

The instrument panel layout is the same in all Alpines, but Series I and II have a gunmetal-coloured moulded Bakelite panel.

Stylish, comfortable, roomy and easy to access. This is a Series 3, still with fins, but with the later windscreen. The handbrake is by the door. (Courtesy Goldsmith family)

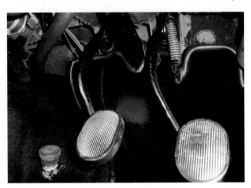

Alpine pedals have 'near' and 'far' settings. Each pedal has alternative holes for its clevis pin. The headlamp dipswitch is conveniently operated by the left foot.

Rootes offered an automatic gearbox option for Series IV only. The selector is neat. (Courtesy Tim Raymond)

Will it fit the garage?
Length: 3.94m/12ft 11in; width: 1.54m/5ft ½in.

Interior space
Whichever Alpine you choose, you will find the cockpit is a nice place to be. Well finished and comfortable, a step up from the 'traditional' British sports car of the

The GT version of the Series 3-V Alpine was supplied with a body-colour hardtop, but as it has no alternative softtop to stow, there is a little more room in the back.
(Courtesy Tim Raymond)

1950s. All cars have an open 'cubby' in the dashboard and a large, lockable centre console. The rear 'seat' can take one adult or two small children – if you are happy about the safety implications. GT models with no soft top have slightly more room around the seat. It's a useful extra luggage and parcels space, too.

Luggage capacity

Series I and II have a fairly small boot (trunk). With the fuel tank in the floor and the spare wheel above it, there's not a lot of room. For Series 3, the boot was redesigned; there's a fuel tank in each wing, and the spare is vertical at the front of the boot. Luggage capacity was doubled by these changes, and these later Alpines have much more room than their competitors.

The Series I and II have limited luggage room because the fuel tank is located in the boot floor, with the spare wheel above.

Series 3-V have double the luggage room. The fuel is in two linked wing tanks, and the spare wheel is mounted in the front of the boot.

Running costs

Modest. Servicing, at nominally 5000 mile intervals, is straightforward, and there's an annual oil and filter change. Some cars have a few greasing points; later models usually have none.

Usability

The Alpine has always been a very usable car. The hardtop, if supplied, makes the Alpine an all-year-round car. However, Alpines were always prone to rust, and if you do use one every day, all year, it will deteriorate. Realistically nowadays, it's a second car, but one that is fine for a European summer tour and, especially with the hardtop, snug in winter.

Parts availability
The Alpine does not have the parts availability enjoyed by Jaguar, MG and Triumph owners. Nevertheless, there are specialists in the UK and the USA (where the majority of Alpines were sold), and they can supply most mechanical parts, plus replica body panels and chrome parts.

The Sunbeam Alpine Owners' Club, which has access to most of the original Rootes drawings, has a policy of providing important parts which are needed but are otherwise unavailable.

Parts costs
See Chapter 2 for a sample list of new parts' costs.

Insurance
Classic car insurers offer very reasonably-priced policies (though the driver's age affects the premium) – but beware of conditions related to leaving cars unattended with the hood (softtop) folded.

Investment potential
Alpines have their place in the classic car lists, and have been neither worse nor better than other cars in the last 25 years. Despite increases in recent times, Alpines are still good value. The downside of this is that if you have to pay someone to undertake a full restoration, you should not then expect to be able to immediately sell the car for a profit.

Foibles
The Rootes family business was supplying well-designed and well-finished cars to its middle-class buyers. Some areas of the car body and fittings are therefore rather complex and time-consuming to get right. Each door and window has 14 possible adjustments for example.

Plus points
Style, relative rarity, a well-balanced and well-engineered design, which is practical, reliable and satisfying to drive.

Minus points
Rust, and because some parts of the structure are complex, they take time (and therefore money) to restore. Minor oil leaks, especially around the crank pulley (there is a fix) are usual. The 1494 and 1592 engines make Alpines a little slower than contemporary MGs.

Alternatives
MGA, MGB, Triumph TR4 or possibly Spitfire, Mazda MX5.

2 Cost considerations
– affordable, or a money pit?

Purchase

The usual advice – 'buy the best you can afford' – applies here. The difficulty lies in judging which is the best, and whether it is as good as it may seem. That's where this book will help you.

The best-quality restoration will probably cost more than the car is then worth. The significance for a buyer is, firstly, if an owner of a top-class car finds that he or she is forced to sell for some reason, a buyer can benefit, and secondly, you should not pay too much for a car needing full restoration.

If you want, and are able to do work yourself, there is more advice in Chapter 13, notably about the all-important structure and corrosion. You may consider paying for the bodyshell to be restored and painted, but then doing mechanical work and the fiddly, time-consuming, but not difficult, assembly of the body fittings and trim yourself.

If all these things are beyond you, or you just want to drive it, then go and find the best.

Servicing

An annual check of the systems tested for the UK's MoT (brakes, suspension, steering, tyres, cooling, electrical items, etc) is a good basis, and is simple to do. You are checking that everything works properly and there are no leaks, wear or corrosion. Oil levels in the gearbox/OD, rear axle and steering should be checked, and the engine oil and filter should be changed every year – when the engine is hot. Antifreeze must be the blue type (not pink), and must be changed every two or three years to ensure that its corrosion-inhibiting properties are maintained. Checks of valve clearances (engine hot), distributor points and carburettors are recommended at 5000 mile intervals.

Spare parts

The Alpine does not have the comprehensive parts supply enjoyed by Jaguar and MG owners, but service parts, such as tyres (165/80 x 13), oil filters, points, brake pads and exhausts are easy to buy.

Most items can be found eventually from UK, US or European suppliers, or secondhand. Note that many mechanical and electrical parts, including some lights, were common to other Rootes vehicles. Harrington-specific trim parts, such as the chrome side flashes, are now effectively impossible to find.

The SAOC has access to the Rootes Archive and hence to most of the factory drawings. Its policy is not to compete with

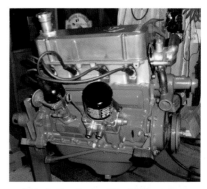

This is the Series V's 1725 engine, identifiable by the dipstick hole in the block, just in front of the distributor. The earlier 3-bearing 1494 and 1592 engine dipsticks fitted into a tube off the sump. (Courtesy Goldsmith family)

established commercial suppliers, but to provision items which are needed, but are otherwise impossible to find.

The tables here are a guide to spares prices, but costs vary between suppliers and with time. Prices shown *exclude* VAT and other taxes.

New mechanical parts

Water hose set	x29
Water pump	x83
Cylinder head gasket	x10
Main bearing set	x69
Conrod bearing set	x66
Valve set	x50
Unleaded head conversion	x250
Fuel pump	x33
Alternator	x75
Distributor	x60
Oil pump	x48
Piston set	x195
Stainless steel exhaust	x350
Radiator (exchange)	x220
Overdrive rebuild	x295
Clutch plate & cover	x120
Clutch master cylinder	x67
Clutch slave cylinder	x47
Propshaft U/J	x13
Brake master cylinder	x112
Brake disc	x56
Brake pad set	x20
Rear slave cylinder	x22
Rear brake shoe set	x28
Upper ball joint	x38
Lower ball joint	x45
SI-3 front suspension kit (1 side)	x225
Trackrod ends (pair)	x49

New replica panels are expensive. It is usual to fit repair sections, as shown here. (Courtesy Tim Raymond)

Body parts

Front wing lower rear section	x68
Rear wing lower front section	x55
Rear wing lower rear section	x108
Inner sill (rocker panel)	x53
Outer sill (rocker panel)	x63
Lower door skin	x44
Seat cover (pair)	x195
Hood (soft top) fabric	x204
Carpet set	x188
Laminated screen	x190

The later Alpines have the same rear lights as Hillmans, Singers and Humbers, and smaller rubber-tipped over-riders. (Courtesy Tim Raymond)

3 Living with an Alpine
– will you get along together?

Alpines are straightforward cars which are practical and good to drive. Regular use is to be encouraged. Cars which are left unused for long periods tend to develop sticking brakes and clutches, and are more likely to suffer corrosion inside the aluminium cylinder head. It's vital to keep fresh corrosion-inhibiting antifreeze in the engine at all times. Another thing to bear in mind is that if you do use your Alpine in salty wet conditions, it will deteriorate.

Performance is adequate – more than adequate if it's a 1725 Series V. The figures on paper don't look too hot, but you will find no problem in today's traffic. In fact, the car responds well to a press-on style, and you may find you overtake more cars than pass you. On motorways, as long as you have overdrive, 70 to 80mph is okay, if a bit noisy. Fuel consumption varies. An Alpine with well-adjusted Strombergs or the modern Weber kit will manage 35mpg touring. A car with a worn Solex may not achieve 25mpg.

Handling is good – better than when new, because you will be running on modern radial tyres, not ancient cross-plies. A tendency to dip the front outer corner on turn-in can be fixed with stiffer or adjustable front shock absorbers, such as Spax. The cooling capacity is just adequate, the worst condition being idle. It is good to fit an electric fan and remove the rather large engine-driven item.

The doors are large and open wide, so access is easy, though it is a low car. Luggage capacity is adequate in Series I and II cars, and generous in later cars. There's internal stowage in the dash, a lockable centre box, and, of course, on the rear seat. Alpine hoods are fiddly by today's standards, but you can be weatherproof in under a minute

Who couldn't live with this view? A Series V GT with wood-rim steering wheel and veneered wood dashboard. The clock and ammeter were extras.

Good access to most things once you lift the forward-hinged bonnet (hood) of this Series V. The heater matrix is under the bonnet lock panel. (Courtesy Bob Standing)

From late Series II, the bonnet (hood) hinges were modified, and the support strut was moved, to improve access.

(30 seconds if the passenger helps). The Series I-II rounded hardtop is aluminium, and light enough to be fitted by one person, but a spanner is needed. The S3-V steel top really requires two people to fit or remove, but takes less than a minute. There are just four over-centre catches.

Unlike modern sports cars, the Alpine does have just enough rear seat room to accommodate one adult or two small children, at least for short journeys. Front seat belts can be fitted to all Alpines – fixed belts were standard on Series V cars. The Securon 264 belt gives you inertia reels. Lap belts for children can be fitted in the rear.

Lights and wipers are the normal 1960s Lucas units. Halogen headlamps are available and easily fitted. The wipers are adequate – though they don't follow the screen's curve at the edges.

Heating and demisting is good – you will always be snug with the roof up, and the heater does help when no roof is present. Series 3-V Alpines have a 2-speed fan.

One feature you will probably miss if you have a modern car is central locking. One key should fit the ignition and doors, and another fits the boot and centre box.

If living with an Alpine means touring, then the later cars' larger boot (trunk) is very useful. (Courtesy Tim Raymond)

A tonneau cover is a useful accessory, especially for a Series 3-V GT which has no softtop. This Series II cover has a 'sausage' which fits into the boot (trunk) gutter.

Do you like the early simple finned shape, with rounded roof ...

... or do you prefer the later cars, with their more angular roof which has better access and visibility, and smaller fins?

4 Relative values
– which model for you?

There are lots of variables which affect values. Prices are affected by buyers' tastes as well as more practical aspects. The finned Series 3 tends to be worth more than the mechanically-similar Series IV which has the later shape. As values in GBP change over time, the values presented here are all shown relative to the most-desirable version – a Series V with overdrive (OD) and both hard and soft tops. Note that this can be a Series V Sports which was supplied with both a hood (soft top) and the optional steel top, or it can be a Series V GT to which the hood has been subsequently added properly.

Other Alpines with OD, a soft hood and a hardtop compare as follows:

Many buyers look for the simple original shape of the Series I or II with rounded corners to doors, bonnet (hood) and boot (trunk), and hidden panel joins all made possible by lead-loading.

Top left: The Series 3 keeps the fins and front grille, but has the larger boot and later screen and roof. (Courtesy Goldsmith family)
Above: For Series IV, the fins were cut down, and the front air intake was revised. (Courtesy Tim Raymond)
Left: At first sight, the Series V appears to be the same as the Series IV but the rounded corners of doors, boot and bonnet have gone, all the panel joins are now visible, and under the bonnet there's a new five-bearing 1725 engine and all-synchro gearbox. (Courtesy Bob Standing)

Series I   80% relative to Series V
Series II   85% relative to Series V
Series 3   95% relative to Series V
Series IV 80% relative to Series V
Series V   100%
Values are about:
• 10% lower if there is no OD
• 3% lower if there is a hood but no hardtop
• 20% lower if there is a hardtop but no hood (Series 3-V GT)
• 5% higher if fitted with *good* factory wire wheels or attractive alloy wheels (non std)
• 2% higher if fitted with an original optional radio and speaker fitting kit.

So the value of a Series IV GT on steel wheels without OD and without a hood is about 60% of the top-spec Series V.

Automatic transmission was a rare option on Series IV Alpines only. Values tend to be a little lower.

Harrington Alpines (and buyers) are really too rare for generalised valuations. Most were based on Series II Alpines; some were on Series 3, and a very few Series IV cars were built. The more elaborate de-finned Harrington Le Mans version may be worth 50% more than a standard Alpine. The simpler Harrington (which retained the fins) attracts at least a 25% premium.

Take care when Alpines are highly priced because they are claimed to have competition history.

The factory-supplied 4.5 x 13in steel wheels with chrome hub-caps and chrome or chrome-aluminium rings. Crossply tyres were originally fitted.

Left: Wire wheels on splined hubs were a factory option. Early cars had 'eared' chrome nuts tightened with a hide hammer; later Alpines had octagonal nuts and a large spanner. Beware of worn splines.
(Courtesy Goldsmith family)
Right: Many cars now have alloy wheels, usually 5.5 x 13in, but 14in can be used with low profile tyres. These are Rootes wheels, made by Exacton for the Avenger Tiger.

A Harrington Alpine Series II. New cars were converted by Harrington in Hove, and supplied – for a much higher price – through the Rootes dealer network, often with Hartwell tuning mods.
(Courtesy Glenn Brackenridge)

The Harrington Le Mans is a more elaborate conversion – with no fins and a full 'hatchback.' This type won the 1961 Le Mans 'Index of Thermal Efficiency.' Owner, Glenn Brackenridge still races his car today.
(Courtesy Glenn Brackenridge)

5 Before you view

– be well informed

To avoid a wasted journey, and the disappointment of finding that the car does not match your expectations, it will help if you're very clear about what questions you want to ask before you pick up the telephone. Some of these points might appear basic but when you're excited about the prospect of buying your dream classic, it's amazing how some of the most obvious things slip the mind ... Also check the current values of the model you are interested in in classic car magazines which give both a price guide and auction results.

Where is the car?

Consider the cost of travelling to view a car. Weigh this against the car's specification. If it's what you want – the correct configuration, Series, etc – it may be worth travelling some distance. However, it is best to view as many Alpines as possible, and local cars can build up your knowledge for little effort and cost, even if you don't buy. It's not out of the question to consider travelling to the sunnier parts of the USA to buy an Alpine. If you want a LHD car this is probably the best course, but you need to identify at least three possible cars and do thorough research – lots of photos, etc – before you buy your air ticket. You also need to research your home country's car import and registration process and costs. As the majority of Alpines were exported, and the British climate has not been kind to those that remained, you are unlikely to find more than about ten Alpines for sale in the UK at any time.

Dealer or private sale

Establish early on if the car is being sold by its owner or by a trader. A private owner should have all the history, so don't be afraid to ask detailed questions. A dealer may have more limited knowledge of a car's history, but should have some documentation. A dealer may offer a warranty/guarantee (ask for a printed copy) and finance – but the price will be higher. There are no specialist Alpine dealers with knowledge worth paying for.

Cost of collection and delivery

A dealer may well be used to quoting for delivery by car transporter. A private owner may agree to meet you halfway, but only agree to this after you have seen the car at the vendor's address to validate the documents. Alternatively, you could meet halfway and agree the sale but insist on meeting at the vendor's address for the handover.

Viewing – when and where?

It is always preferable to view at the vendor's home or business premises. In the case of a private sale, the car's documentation should tally with the vendor's name and address. Arrange to view only in daylight and avoid a wet day. Most cars look better in poor light or when wet.

Reason for sale

Do make it one of the first questions. Why is the car being sold and how long has it been with the current owner? How many previous owners?

This is very important. Five or more years' ownership and use, with paper history and photographs of work done, is good. An 'older restoration' which still looks good has proved its worth. Be very cautious with less than two years' ownership and no history, or a succession of short-term owners.

Conversions and specials

Some Alpines have been returned to the UK from the USA or other kinder climates. Most of these will have been built as LHD, and some will have been converted to RHD. The bodyshells were identical, so it is possible to do a perfect conversion, but the chassis plate will always reveal the car's true origin. The conversion requires at least a RHD steering box, dashboard, handbrake, hydraulic pipes, headlamps and pedals, and really ought to have a new wiring loom and revised wiper mechanism.

Many Series 3-V GT Alpines have been converted to have the Tourer hood and stowage assembly. This is a very desirable conversion, as long as it is done well. You get the GT's steel top, veneered wood dashboard, wood-rim steering wheel, carpets and better door trims and cappings, plus the flexibility afforded by the built-in hood.

There are aftermarket fibreglass hardtops for Series 3-V Alpines. These look similar to the Rootes steel items, and they don't rust, but are not as desirable as the original.

The Solex B32 carburettor used on Series IV and some Series 3 Alpines

The author's non-standard softtop stowage on his converted Series V GT. Note Securon 264 seat belts.

Tourer door trims are plain vynide, with visible painted metal all round. This is a Series II, with a single full-height pillar at the front to guide the door glass. The SI is similar, though the pillar is just a stub.

GT Alpines have trims which cover almost all the door and have a welded pattern. There are black cappings above the trims. Series 3-V cars have these fixed quarterlights. The lower casting of the GT quarterlight is shaped to match the door capping. Tourers have a simpler part. The window winder was moved higher up the door for Series V.

was not the best, and it worsens with age. A Weber 28/36 will fit the same manifold, but the best solution is the new manifold and Weber 32/36 DGV, with remote air filter, developed specially for the Alpine and related vehicles. It's also a good alternative to worn out Zeniths or Strombergs.

Some Alpine Series I to IV have been fitted with the later Series V 1725 engine. If the original head and carburettors are used, it is hardly noticeable (the dipstick goes directly into the block). The usual source for a 1725 is an Arrow range vehicle (Hunter, Vogue, Rapier, Iranian Paykan, etc) made between 1966 and about 1980, but it has to have been built with the aluminium head (the valve order with iron head is different), and the Alpine manifolds, water pump and engine mountings must be used. It's quicker and more durable – but not original. You will have to decide if it's what you want.

Similarly, some early Alpines now have the later all-synchro gearbox. (The Arrow gearbox does not fit an Alpine, though many internal parts are the same.)

There are Alpines around with (or claimed to have) 'Holbay' engines. This version of the 1725 motor was introduced after the end of Alpine production, and only ever fitted to 'Arrow' range Rapier H120 and Hunter GLS saloons,

This Series IV automatic has the recently-developed manifold and Weber 32/36 DGV kit. (Courtesy Tim Raymond)

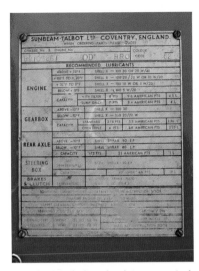

The Series II chassis plate, mounted on the scuttle panel, also tells the owner which oils to use.

Series I and II cars built at the Armstrong Siddeley Parkside factory in Coventry should also have a body number plate.

between 1968 and 1975. The Holbay had a modified cylinder head with smaller inlet ports, flat-top pistons to counter the enlarged combustion chamber volume, a wilder camshaft and twin Weber 40 DCOE carburettors. As the Arrow range had engines tilted to the right, the Holbay manifolds do not fit the Alpine, though the inlet can be cut and welded. The Holbay engine produced about 110bhp, compared with the Series V's normal 88bhp. It is common to keep the Stromberg carburettors to avoid the difficulties of installing the twin Webers.

The Holbay does produce more power but it is less tractable than the standard engine.

To be certain that a car has a genuine Holbay, you really have to ensure that the inlet ports are small, the pistons have flat tops, and the cam lift is correct. It is very easy to fit a Holbay rocker cover to a standard motor.

Condition

Ask for an honest appraisal of the car's condition. Ask specifically about some of the check items described in Chapter 7.

All original specification

Originality is normally best. However, a 'GT' with a properly fitted Tourer soft top or an early Alpine with the later 1725 engine, may be seen as more desirable by many buyers. 'Customising' generally lowers value.

Matching data/legal ownership

Do VIN/chassis, engine numbers and licence plate match the official registration document? Is the owner's name and address recorded in the official registration documents?

For those countries that require an annual test of roadworthiness (eg, an MoT certificate in the UK), does the car have a document showing it complies?

If a smog/emissions certificate is mandatory, does the car have one?

If required, does the car carry a current road fund licence/licence plate tag? All Alpines are exempt from UK road tax, but cars must have an annual registration or, if not in use, a SORN.

Alpines have numbers in several places. There will be a chassis plate on the bonnet-locking platform showing the car's chassis number, plus letters indicating LHD, RHD, OD if fitted, GT (if it was a GT) and a colour code. The numbers on Series IV-V plates were stamped from behind. The chassis number also indicates the car's Series (see Chapter 17).

The engine should also have a number on the block just forward of the oil filter, facing upwards. Originally, this number will have been the same as the chassis number. It's not unusual for Alpines to have later been given a block from a related Rootes saloon. Engines from Sunbeam Rapiers and Humber Sceptres were similar or identical to the Alpine version, and are therefore fine if the car's registration documents reflect the change, but lesser cars had cast iron cylinder heads with a different valve order. An Alpine with an iron head is not a good buy – unless you have a correct engine waiting.

There should be a body number on a painted steel tag near the chassis number. This will begin SAL and be followed by digits.

The SAOC can often assist with identifying an Alpine's origin and configuration, and with dating. Non-members pay a charge.

Does the vendor own the car outright? Money might be owed to a finance company or bank: the car could even be stolen. Several organisations will supply the data on ownership, based on the car's licence plate number, for a fee. Such companies can often also tell you whether the car has been 'written-off' by an insurance company. In the UK these organisations can supply vehicle data via their websites or on these numbers:

HPI – 01722 422 422
AA – 0800 316 3564
DVLA – 0300 790 6802
RAC – 0330 159 0364

Other countries will have similar organisations.

Series 3 Alpines have three plates. The large one is a data plate with oil types, etc. Next to it is the chassis plate, which also shows the model, OD if overdrive is fitted, and the colour code. At the top of this photo is the small plate with the SAL number – applied by Pressed Steel Fisher who made the later bodies in Cowley. (Courtesy Goldsmith family)

Saving a few pennies by leaving off the data plate means that Series V owners have to search the handbook for data.

Roadworthiness
All but early Alpine Series I cars made in 1959 will require a current MoT certificate if used in the UK.

Status can be checked on-line at www.gov.uk/check-mot-status, or by calling 0845 600 5977. Recent MoT history can be seen at www.check-mot.service.gov.uk/.

Unleaded fuel

The engines will run satisfactorily on 95 octane unleaded fuel for a while, but will eventually suffer valve seat recession. Heads can be converted by changing the exhaust valve seats, and preferably by installing bronze valve guide liners (to prevent sticking). The valves are fine.

Unleaded fuel additives have been suspected of loosening the paint used inside Alpine fuel tanks to form a fine dust which will block carburettor jets.

Ethanol can cause problems for Alpine (and all other old car) owners, though it is too early to be certain about every aspect. At the current average 5% (in the UK) it will dissolve old deposits in tanks and fuel lines. It is more prone to vaporisation – especially where the delivery pipe passes close to the thermostat housing. Ethanol may eventually attack brass and zinc parts in the carburettors and fuel pump, and the nylon fuel pipe used from Series 3 onwards. E10 (10% Ethanol), if adopted, is expected to make matters worse. The SAOC and the FBHVC are monitoring the situation.

Insurance

Check with your existing insurer before setting out, your current policy might not cover you to drive the car.

How you can pay

A cheque/check will take several days to clear and the seller may prefer to sell to a cash buyer. However, a banker's draft (a cheque issued by a bank) is a good as cash, but safer, so contact your own bank and become familiar with the formalities that are necessary to obtain one. An on-line bank transfer may be the best solution, and is increasingly likely to be preferred.

Buying at auction?

If the intention is to buy at auction see Chapter 10 for further advice.

Professional vehicle check

Alpines are not complex cars by today's standards. Nevertheless, there are some important checks that should be made. If you feel unsure about making these checks yourself, you may be able to persuade another competent owner to assist (the SAOC in the UK, or other owners' clubs elsewhere may be able to put you in touch). There are also organisations in the UK which will carry out a general professional check. Contact them via their websites or these numbers:

AA – 0800 056 8040 (motoring organisation with vehicle inspectors)
RAC – 0330 159 0720 (motoring organisation with vehicle inspectors)

Other countries will have similar organisations.

6 Inspection equipment
– these items will really help

Before you rush out of the door, gather together a few items that will help as you work your way around the car:

This book
Reading glasses (if you need them for close work)
Magnet (not powerful, a fridge magnet is ideal)
Torch
Trolley jack AND axle stand(s)
Probe (a small screwdriver works very well)
Overalls
Mirror on a stick
Digital camera
GPS speedometer (smartphone app)
A friend, preferably a knowledgeable enthusiast

Your car-viewer's kit – the digital camera is not shown because it was in use! Note the free GPS speedometer app on my phone.

This book is designed to be your guide at every step, so take it along and use the check boxes in Chapter 9 to help you assess each area of the car you're interested in. Don't be afraid to let the seller see you using it.

Take your reading glasses if you need them to read documents and make close-up inspections.

A magnet will help you check if the car is full of filler, or has fibreglass panels. Use the magnet (wrapped in thin cloth to avoid scratches) to sample bodywork areas all around the car, but be careful not to damage the paintwork. Expect to find a little filler here and there, but not whole panels. Fibreglass panels have been made for Alpines in the past. If made and painted well, bonnets and boot lids are fine, but the car will be weakened with fibreglass wings.

A torch with fresh batteries will be useful for peering into the wheelarches and under the car.

A small screwdriver can be used – with care – as a probe, particularly in the wheelarches and on the underside. With this you should be able to check an area of severe corrosion, but be careful – if it's really bad the screwdriver might go right through the metal!

Be prepared to get dirty. Take along a pair of overalls, if you have them. Fixing a mirror at an angle on the end of a stick may seem odd, but you'll probably need it to check the condition of the underside of the car. It will also help you to peer into some of the important crevices. You can also use it, together with the torch, along the underside of the sills and on the floor.

Take photographs so that later you can study some areas of the car more closely. Take a picture of any part of the car that causes you concern, and seek an expert's opinion.

Ideally, have a friend or knowledgeable enthusiast accompany you: a second opinion is always valuable.

7 Fifteen minute evaluation
– walk away or stay?

Before you even get close to the car, walk around it and have a look at the fit of the doors and sills. These are difficult to restore well if the structure is rusty, so their fit and appearance are usually a good guide to how well any work has been done. Look closely at the seams between the wings and sills, etc. These were all hidden (by lead) on Series I cars but, eventually, most were later left visible to save money (see Chapter 17). Check whether your car is correct against the photographs in this book. Check that the lower edges of the doors sit flush when closed, and don't stick out. Also check that the lower edges of the doors and both top and bottom of the sills are curved when viewed side-on – higher front and rear than between.

Check whether the doors open and close smoothly, and whether the windows wind properly – they can become stiff, then winder mechanisms get overloaded and can wear or fail.

Open the bonnet and inspect the engine bay for poor wiring or other DIY 'bodges.' Is the external paint the same colour as under the bonnet and in the boot, and is it the original colour? (The paint code is on the chassis plate; Chapter 17 lists Alpine codes and colours). Check the engine number. Is it the same as the chassis number, or is the engine at least the same type?

Check that the car has an aluminium cylinder head. When Alpines were almost worthless, a few owners fitted Hillman Minx engines with iron heads. Walk away unless you know where to find the correct engine.

Is the car what the seller claims? Does it have all the right features for its Series (see tables in Chapter 17)? If there are modifications, have they been installed well, and are they acceptable to you?

Start by looking at the fit of the panels, especially around the doors. Note the curved lower edge to the door and sill. Most seams were covered on a Series 3. (Courtesy Goldsmith family)

Square corners and visible seams on a Series V.

Square corners to the boot lid, '1725' badges, and wood dashboard and steering wheel make this a Series V GT. (Courtesy Tim Raymond)

Twin Zeniths and a large header tank are to be found under the Series II bonnet.

Left: Round corner to the bonnet and no visible seam is correct up to series IV. Right: Square corner and a visible scuttle seam on this Series V. (Courtesy Tim Raymond)

All Alpines have aluminium cylinder heads. The sparkplugs were in round tubes up to early Series V.

Revised sidelamps and air intake for Series IV. The SUNBEAM letters were deleted for Series V. (Courtesy Tim Raymond)

Later 1725 engines have rectangular recesses around the sparkplugs. (Courtesy Goldsmith family)

Now check the interior. Lift the front carpets or mats and check for damp and rust. Is the dashboard in good condition with the correct instruments? A clock (centre) and an ammeter (extreme right in a RHD car) were optional extras replacing matching blanks. Have extra holes been drilled for switches, etc?

Check that the car has the correct gearbox. Series I to early Series IV (chassis numbers B940 ...) should have a gearbox with synchromesh on second, third and fourth. Reverse will be left-and-back, next to second. Later Series IV and all Series V (chassis numbers B941 ... and B395 ...) have all-synchro gearboxes and reverse will be right-and-back, next to fourth.

Does the car have overdrive (OD)? There will be a column stalk on the right of Series I-3, and on the left in later cars (RHD). If it doesn't have OD, does the chassis plate

This is a Series 3 Tourer, but the owner has added a wooden dashboard, wood-rim wheel and wooden gear knob. (Courtesy Goldsmith family)

Reverse is left-and-back on the Series I-IV gearbox (with no synchromesh on first).

The overdrive relay (a special type for Series 3-V) is mounted on the right side of the bulkhead. Original RHD brake master cylinders have an integral cast reservoir.

Convenient safe hardtop storage. The rear edge rests on a shelf; the front is held up by a swinging hook. This ex-Tiger hardtop has a factory-fitted Webasto sunroof which makes the roof heavy.

suggest that it was supplied with OD? If so, it will have a lower rear axle ratio and will need OD. Turn on the ignition – don't start the engine – and check that the OD engages and disengages in third and fourth (you can hear clicks from the relay and solenoid), but not in first, second or reverse.

Check the seats – tip each one forward and look underneath at the rubber diaphragms on Series 3-V. Series I-II seats only adjust F/A, but Series 3-V seats have adjustable squabs with a lock lever at the side.

The top of each sill seam should be covered by a furflex plastic trim, NOT a seal. Each door should have a seal in a channel along its bottom and rear edges. People repairing rusty doors don't always bother to replace the channels. A seal on the sill top will tend to push the door outwards at the bottom. (Even otherwise correct modern seals which are too stiff may do this, too.)

Check the boot floor and the lower rear wings for rust. If there's a hardtop, inspect that for damage and, if it's the later factory steel top, check carefully for rust, looking underneath it when off the car. All hardtop windows are Perspex.

If the car has a hood, check that it folds and unfolds correctly, and that the stowage arrangements work properly. When 'up' look at the fit of the fabric, and check for tears, etc.

Now start the engine. If it's cold, it may not spin very fast – it's large for the type of starter motor fitted – but it should start with some choke. Watch the oil pressure. When cold, it should come up immediately to at least 50psi. When hot, and above 2000rpm, the pressure in the 1494 and 1592 engines should be 50psi, whereas the 1725 runs at 40psi.

After all the above, you can now go for a drive. The car may be a bit temperamental when cold, but fine once warm. You should be able to engage all gears easily and smoothly, except for the non-synchromesh first gear on earlier cars. This can only be easily engaged when stationary. In each gear, accelerate to about 4000rpm, then lift off and slow down to check that it doesn't jump out of gear. Note that over-reading electronic tachometers on Series 3-V are common. Check the speedometer against a GPS, if possible.

The servoed brakes on Series 3-V should be light and powerful; Series I-II brakes will work but need more effort. A *very slight* pull to one side under braking (only) is not uncommon. Steering may be heavy when parking, but easier on the move.

Test the OD, if fitted. You will need to dip the clutch briefly for smoothness, especially when disengaging. Engagement should be almost immediate with no 'slip' thereafter.

8 Key points

– where to look for problems

The first priority is to establish exactly what is being offered – the original Series and specification, and all subsequent changes and modifications. Then the vital aspects of condition. Items to check are:

• Ownership history. Few owners and long-term ownership is good. Full history and photos of work done are desirable. Be wary if there have been lots of owners, restoration is very recent, and documentation is sparse.

• Chassis and engine numbers, and engine type. If the numbers don't match, is the engine the correct type? Has a 1725 been fitted to an earlier car? Has it an aluminium cylinder head?

Non-standard – though well done. This Series 3 has a Holbay engine complete with the twin 40DCOE Webers squeezed in on a cut-and-welded Hunter GLS inlet manifold. The owner has kept the original cast alloy rocker cover rather than fit the 'Holbay' item. (Courtesy Goldsmith family)

Nothing wrong with the fit and finish of this Series II door and sill.

Above: This Series IV looked quite good, but behind the rusty outer sill were rusty inner and intermediate sills.
Right: Underside of the same car later on after extensive sill and floor repairs.
(Courtesy Tim Raymond)

Pull back the carpet here, and under the seats to check the floors. The 'V' knob controls the footwell vents (Series V only).

• Bodyshell specification – round or square corners on doors, bonnet and boot? Visible seams where appropriate.
• Door fits. Do the bottom edges of the sills and doors have the correct curve? Do the doors stick out at the rear lower corner?
• Corrosion. Check sills, rear arches (inner and outer), rear chassis boxes, main members underfloor, floors, front chassis legs.
• Quality of structural repairs. Is it metal or filler? Beware of underseal, especially if new. Is the paint finish good, free of blistering and blemishes?
• Interior trim. Is there damp? Are the seats damaged? Are the foams and diaphragms still supportive? Is the dashboard in good condition?
• Poor quality restoration or modifications in the engine bay. Are pipes well fitted? Are there extra wires and fuses? Has the work been well done?
• Soft and hard tops. Do they fit, especially around the door glasses? Are the hardtop perspex windows good? If it's a later steel top, is it rusty?

Some creasing in the rear quarters is normal for the later softtops. (Courtesy Goldsmith family)

9 Serious evaluation

– 60 minutes for years of enjoyment

You will be buying an Alpine because you want one, not because it exactly fits your transport needs, and if you examine several Alpines, as you should, it's hard to remember the exact details of each. This chapter tries to bring some objectivity to this unreliable, subjective and emotional process. Not only will it help you decide *which* car to buy, it can also help you identify 'bargaining points' when it comes to pricing. The sections are specifically tailored to the Alpine – their particular weaknesses and the all-important differences between Series. Mark (or ask your friend to mark) each section Excellent (4), Good (3), Average (2), or Poor (1), being as realistic as possible. Use your magnet and small probe when checking for rust.

General appearance and fit

Look carefully at the car from each side, then from the front and rear. Does it 'sit' well? Are the bonnet and boot fits and gaps good? Most importantly, do the doors fit well? Are the bumpers straight and well aligned? Do the door front channels and glasses meet the screen and roof (or roofs) accurately? Is the car level when viewed from behind?

Care is needed to make the glasses fit well against the hood frame seals.

The door glasses overlap the front of the later hardtop windows, and the top edges fit closely against the top seals.

All seems straight and good at the front of this Series 3. It has the bonnet badge which was deleted on Series IV. These large bulbous over-riders were standard on Series I-3. (Courtesy Goldsmith family)

Front valance and bumper mounts
The valance and the horizontal panel above are easily damaged, and are prone to rust. Check for dents, corrosion, cracks around the starting handle hole and general 'fit.' Check the two anchor nuts which are number-plate bracket mountings. The bumper mounts on two brackets which bolt into the ends of the chassis legs. Below each bolt is a square socket for the jack. Check for rust and damage or poor repairs.

New lights and intake trim for the Series IV. No bonnet badge, but it keeps the SUNBEAM letters. The inside of the intake is painted black – often forgotten by restorers. (Courtesy Tim Raymond)

Sills (rocker panels)

The Alpine has three layers of deep sills. They are vital parts of the structure, and are expensive to replace. The seams where they join the front and rear wings were covered with lead on early cars, but were left visible on later Series IV and all Series V. The sill and door bottom edges should be curved – lower in the middle than at the front or rear. Some replacement sills were made with straight edges. These don't then match the door bottoms. Try to check the stiffness of the structure. The best way is to jack the car under the front eye of a rear spring until the wheel is off the ground, then have someone try to move the rear bumper up and down while you observe the gap at the top of the door. An alternative is to use the original jack at the rear and see if the gap closes. At the very least, with the car on the ground, you should have someone try to move the bumper up and down while you observe the door gap. Movement up to about 2mm is normal; much more than that, or evidence of door contact means the car is weak.

New sill and rear wing repair section on a Series 3. The joint was hidden by lead loading. (Courtesy Goldsmith family)

Floors

Check the front and rear floors by lifting carpets or mats, and tipping the seats forward. Look for rust, repairs and water ingress – which will result in corrosion later. If the car is wet at the front of the gearbox tunnel, the heater drain hose (or the footwell vent drain hoses on Series V) may be disconnected. Check the seat mountings – they bolt to F/A boxes – and especially check the inner sill faces and the floor joins, and the area in front of and above the rear spring eyes.

The inner and outer rear wheelarches contribute to the Alpine's strength and stiffness. They join the sill assembly to the box sections which are further inboard, and which carry the rear springs. (Courtesy Tim Raymond)

Series 3-V cars have a false floor in the passenger's footwell. There is another 6in of lost legroom beyond, though the bulkhead slopes backwards.

You won't see all this when you go and view a car, but this is what it should be like – in this case after fairly extensive restoration. (Courtesy Goldsmith family)

Rear wheelarches

These are important because they join the sills to the rear chassis legs which carry the springs and are further inboard. They also carry the seatbelt mount upper anchorages (from Series 3). Pay extra attention to these and the entire arch forward and below the anchorages. Look for signs of repair. Be suspicious of thick layers of underseal.

Look carefully at the wheelarch flanges. They corrode from inside and it is common to find repairs here. The join between the wing and the inner arch is important.

Underneath   4 3 2 1

NOTE: Whenever you go underneath a car, you MUST ensure that it is properly supported. A jack or bricks are NOT safe. A ramp, pit or axle stand is needed.

You will find the deep X-shaped member centred just behind the gearbox, with box-sections going to each front corner. You are also likely to find oil – almost all cars leak a little from the engine or gearbox. The oil usually protects the central areas, but look for rust as you move outboard. Particularly check:
• the sill/X box joins at the front and sides
• the small boxes nearby which were used to support the shell during assembly
• the whole length of the chassis members over the rear axle and their spring hangars
• the front chassis legs, especially near the bumper mounts

Look for damage to the X box sections. They are the lowest part of the car, so some knocks are inevitable.

Examine the joint where the large front crossmember is bolted up to the chassis legs. There are aluminium tapered spacers which tilt the suspension to set the required castor angle. If you can see white corrosion products, new ones are probably needed.

The view aft from below the radiator. Note the exhaust routing through the chassis box section – a source of rattles and bangs if not carefully set up. Brake and fuel lines and the speedometer cable are on the left. There should be lots of wax in the box sections at the sides.
(Courtesy Tim Raymond)

The underside view from the rear of this Series V. The fuel line runs under the centre of the boot floor, then round the spare wheel well. This car's rear springs are wrapped in fabric tape. Telescopic rear shock absorbers are fitted on all but Series I and II. The main silencer is left and forward of the differential, except on Series I. There is a further tailpipe silencer.
(Courtesy Tim Raymond)

The complex understructure showing the basic Husky floor, with the added 'X' bracing boxes that link with the front of the sill, and the box sections that go forward and carry the front suspension.
(Courtesy Goldsmith family)

It's convenient at this point to check the brake pipe and fuel line which pass along the car, right of centre.

If it's a Series I or II, check the exposed fuel tank for corrosion and leaks.

Exhaust

While checking the structure, you should also look at the exhaust. It passes through the box section and is prone to touching it. There are lots of joints. Mounts are just behind the 'X,' over the rear axle, and there are two at the rear of the system. All cars have a tailpipe silencer; all but early models also have a larger box next to the diff. Many cars have stainless steel systems now.

Series I-II had a fabricated exhaust manifold. Most later cars have a twin downpipe cast manifold, but Series 3 GTs had just a single pipe. Some people fit fabricated manifolds to later cars.

Door structures

As already mentioned, the general fit of Alpine doors is usually a good indication of the state of the car's structure and the quality of any repairs. They should not only be visually good, but also open and close easily. When the lower parts of the doors weaken through rust, the doors twist and the rear lower corners protrude. It takes care to put things right. The bottoms of each door should have a seal carried in a C channel along the bottom and up the rear edge.

Check also the front face around the hinges and the panel above.

A reminder that the seal should be in a channel on the door, not on the sill.

There should be an oval access hole, filled with a rubber bung, below each front and rear glass channel, and there should be drain holes. There should NOT be a seal along the top edge of the sill and up the triangular 'fillet.' This seam should be covered with plastic trim only. A seal here will tend to twist the door and make it hard to close.

Door fittings

As the doors are long and heavy, the hinges tend to wear. Check by trying to move the rear of the door up and down while partly open. They can be re-pinned. The straps should 'click' and hold the door open. Operate the window winders. If the doors have not been adjusted correctly they may be stiff, and this leads to wear and failure (there are repair kits for Series 3-V). Check also that the door glasses, when raised, are securely held and don't rattle. Check the chromed surround of each door lock for cracks, and check the adjustable strikers on the body for excessive wear.

Rear wings (fenders) and valance

The wings are likely to have repair panels to the rear of the wheels. These join to vertical pieces alongside the rear spring shackles. Check for rust, and for the shape and fit. The rear valance is less prone to rust unless the boot floor fails. Check the jacking points – ideally by using the car's own jack.

Boot (trunk) lid, floor and fuel tank(s)

Lift the mat and check for rust or repairs, especially at the side and rear edges. If it's a Series I or II, check the fuel tank for rust or leaks. Look underneath around the tank 'sender.' If it's a Series 3-V, look into the rear lamp access holes in the trim for

Far left: The Series I-II fuel tank lies below the spare wheel in the boot floor. Left: The Series I-II fuel tank is vulnerable to road dirt and salt. The contents sender is at the rear.

signs or smells of leaks. If you are suspicious, ask if you can remove the side trim boards to see the tanks. There should be a cross-breather rubber tube passing below the boot hinges.

Check the areas where the boot stays are mounted for rust or damage. There are powerful springs to keep the boot lid raised.

Check the rear lower part of the boot lid for rust.

Left: Series 3-V Alpines have a tank in each wing. They are isolated from road dirt. The filler connects to the right tank, and the sender is in the top of this left side tank. The tanks are normally covered by millboard trims.
Right: The right side tank and, just painted but not refitted, the large pipes which pass through the rear of the car and link the two tanks. Short rubber pipes join the tanks and the three joining pipes. (Courtesy Goldsmith family)

Front wings (fenders)

The front wings were made from three main parts - the headlamp surround and top front section, the main central section, and the top rear 'horn' – which were welded and leaded before assembly. Look for rust (or poor repairs) around the headlamp, at the join with the valance, and everywhere below the 'Alpine' chrome script, especially down the line where the inner arch joins on the inside. The arch was not joined mechanically, but it should be sealed to the wing with mastic.

Scuttle

The outer scuttle panel can rust where it lies on an inner panel. Spot-welds, just in front of the screen, becoming 'dimples' are signs that this is occurring. It is a difficult panel to repair – the screen has to be removed. On later Series IV and V cars, the seams where the scuttle joins the wings should be visible.

Paint

If you are following this chapter in sequence you will by now have looked at most of the paint on the car. What colour is the car? Is it the original colour indicated on the chassis plate (many Alpines have been changed, usually to red)? If it isn't *the* original colour, is it *an* original colour (see table in Chapter 17)? Is it the same colour everywhere – under the scuttle, in the engine bay, inside the rear wings, etc? And is it a colour you like or want? If there is a hardtop, is it the same colour (or black)?

Is the paint itself good? Are there rust bubbles? Is there micro-blistering? Does it all match? Is there evidence of poor masking when it was applied?

Windscreen (windshield)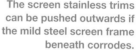

Series I-II cars have a chromed brass screen assembled from four pieces. Later cars have an assembly of mild-steel pressings covered with four stainless trims. The pressings rust, and the evidence is usually that the trims are forced outwards where they meet near the bottom corners. Pushing the top centre of the screen with the roof down may help assessment of any weakness. Look for screen damage – especially scratches from worn or damaged blades. The original toughened screen may have been replaced by a laminated part. Minor delamination along the side edges is common.

Wipers should park on the passenger's side (therefore different for LHD and RHD).

The screen stainless trims can be pushed outwards if the mild steel screen frame beneath corrodes.

Lights, body fittings and trim

Check each light in turn for function, cracks in lenses and poor chrome. Rear lights on Series I-3 were unique to the Alpine. Front sidelamps on Series IV-V were unique to the Alpine and Tiger. Other lights are more common. Halogen headlamp conversions are common (and worthwhile). The cast peaked headlamp surrounds were always body-coloured. Smaller un-peaked rings were fitted to very late Series V. Don't forget the map light above the glove pocket (Series 3 on) and the main light on the screen of GT cars.

The Series I-3 grille, round sidelights, trim, bumper and over-rider.

Then check each badge and handle, etc. All Alpines have SUNBEAM letters on the boot lid and Alpine 'scripts' on the front wings. Series 3-V have shield badges below the scripts and on the right side of the boot. All but Series V have SUNBEAM letters above the air intake, and Series I-3 also have a round badge on the bonnet.

Series I-3 have a chromed grille in the front intake; Series IV-V have a single bar with a central oval badge They also have

Series IV and V cars have a central cross-bar (with an oval badge), and upper and lower trims. The intake is painted matt black behind the trims. The later over-riders are smaller and are rubber-tipped. All Alpines had body-coloured headlamp trims. The last few Series V have smaller unpeaked trims.

Above: The Series I-3 fin and rear lamp (unique to the Alpine). This is a Series II. The filler is located higher up on a Series 3.
Right: The later cars have lower fins with revised rear lamps. Note the Series IV–V flip-top filler cap.

a stainless strip below, on the top of the valance. The strip is often missing, as is matt black paint behind this strip and in the air intake as a whole. This is a possible indication of lack of knowledge or care on the part of whoever restored the car.

Front and rear bumpers are identical (except for a few early cars, and the very last Series Vs which had number-plate lights added). Series I-3 have large bulged over-riders; later cars have smaller rubber-tipped items. Some restorers fit new repro stainless-steel bumpers.

The door handles have spring-loaded lock covers. There should be one key of the doors and ignition, and another for the boot and centre box.

Soft top and hardtop

Soft tops were fitted to all Alpines except Series 3-V GT models. Hard tops (in body colour) were only supplied as standard with Series 3-V GTs. Other buyers could order a black hardtop as an 'extra.' The first consideration here is whether the car has the configuration you want.

Series I-II screens, door glasses and tops are completely different from Series 3-V. There are NO common or mixable parts.

Only early Series I cars have triangular rear quarter windows in the soft top – they were deleted as the material is creased when stowed.

The later soft tops have fixed cantrails with rubber seals for the door glasses. Series I-II cantrails were clipped on, and can be lost.

4 3 2 1

Series 3-V have larger side windows than earlier cars, and there are full frames and seals for the door windows. (Courtesy Goldsmith family)

The soft tops of Series I-IV are stowed away behind three folding steel panels. Care is needed to prevent the sharp corners of the side panels damaging the fabric. The hood can be a tight fit in the stowage, especially if fabric that is thicker than the original vinyl is used.

Series I-IV soft tops were stowed behind folding steel boxes; the Series V top stowed behind a fixed 'wall' with a soft vinyl cover. Many GTs have had a soft top fitted by a later owner, usually with the appropriate stowage arrangement, but some owners have tried other schemes, sometimes to make the soft top assembly detachable so they can keep the GT rear trim.

Raise the soft top and check for tears, rips, fading and discolouration of the rear window. Also check the general fit, especially at the top rear of the doors. It is rare to find an Alpine without minor creasing in the rear quarter area. Check the fit of the door glasses against the seals on Series 3-V.

The Series I-II hardtops were aluminium with a very curved shape and wrap-around rear window. Later hardtops were steel and more angular, with rear side windows. All hardtop windows were Perspex, and these suffer crazing eventually. The Series 3-V rear window was originally curved in both senses, but modern replacements are usually made from flat sheet and only curve across the car.

All hardtops are properly lined inside. Check the later tops for rust at the base of the rear pillars and the frames forward of there. There should be rubber seals in channels around the underside of the rear part. Check the various catches and fittings.

Hood neatly stowed away. Series V cars have a different system. The vertical 'wall' is fixed, and the top is a three-piece flexible cover, like the back part of a tonneau.

Inside the cockpit   4 3 2 1

You are looking at general quality and fit, and to see if there are items missing. Also, check to see if things have been added, and if so whether they are appropriate and well done.

The black padded trim above the dashboard often lifts slightly from the scuttle underneath, and may eventually crack, especially in hot climates.

All Alpines had carpet on the gearbox tunnel and at the sides; Tourers came with rubber floor mats and GTs with carpets. Nowadays, most cars have carpets everywhere.

Series I-II Alpine dashboards were finished in gunmetal grey; Series 3-V Tourers had black plastic dashboards.

Series 3-V GTs had superior fittings; a wood-rim wheel in place of black plastic, a wood-veneered dashboard, black door cappings (with matching modified chrome quarterlights), better door trims which leave no exposed paint and which have a line pattern welded on, a token rear seat cushion, and vinyl trims around the rear seat area with padded cappings.

Series I and II seats are plain and simple. Beware of rusty or broken tubular frames or collapsed foam. Series 3-V seats are based on a Microcell design, and have adjustable backrests.

Rootes supplied a radio console, with speaker below, as an accessory. Check the trims to see if other holes for speakers have been cut.

All cars have an ashtray behind the gearlever and a centre box. The glove pocket in the dash (which was never supplied with a lid) has a Bakelite surround – check it for cracks. Alpine pedals can be set in two positions. The brake and clutch have two clevis-pin holes; the accelerator pedal has two floor positions. Check where they are set, and whether it's right for you.

Adjust the seats, F/A on all Series and the backrest in Series 3-V. Also set the steering wheel – see next section.

Instruments, switches and warning lights

The Alpine's battery lives under the rear seat, on the right side. It should have a hinged cover.

Rootes used Lucas switches and Smiths/Jaeger instruments. Blanks were fitted in the centre and at the extreme end of the driver's side of the dash. A clock and ammeter were accessories which could be bought to fit in place of the blanks. Clocks are desirable but often unreliable. Series 3-V have red instrument needles in place of white. A cigar lighter could replace another small blank next to the glove pocket.

Series 3-V Alpines have an adjustable steering column – it can be moved F/A after unscrewing the centre boss. The indicator and overdrive switches were different from Series I-II. Check both carefully.

Also check the horn ring for cracks, repairs and function.

Check to see if holes for extra switches have been cut.

The warning lights of Series 3-V have tiny drop-down shades to dim the lights at night.

Check the heater controls

Left: Series I and II tools – a jack, handle/wheelbrace and a starting handle.
Right: The jack fits in the square socket at each corner. The wheelbrace also facilitates up and down movement.

move smoothly, and actually move the water valve under the bonnet and the flap under the heater. Check that the fan switch works. For Series I-3 you pull out the air-distribution control lever. Later cars have a normal switch.

If the car has the optional overdrive, now is a good time to check out the switching. With the ignition turned on, the column switch should have no effect if the gearlever is kept in the first-second plane. In third or fourth, you should hear a 'clonk' from below the car when OD is engaged, and a further click when either the column switch is raised, or you move the gearlever left across to second or first. Series I-II cars will re-engage OD if you move the lever back to third or fourth (assuming the switch is still in the engaged position); Series 3-V cars will not re-engage OD until the column switch is again moved down.

Wipers have one speed on Series I-II, two on later cars. All cars have manual screenwashers, but don't be surprised to find a power conversion.

Don't forget to check the floor-mounted headlamp dipswitch.

Electrical system and looms

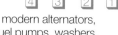

Many Alpines have had modifications, and it is common to find modern alternators, cooling fans, ignition systems, relays, fuses, alarms, air-horns, fuel pumps, washers, radios, etc. Only you can decide if you like the changes, but the important thing is whether the work has been done well. Check if extra wires are neatly bound into a loom and whether proper 'Lucar' or bullet connectors have been used – not 'Scotchloks.' If fuses have been added, does the seller know which fuse protects which circuit?

Series I-IV cars originally had the usual Lucas dynamo and control box and were positive earth. Series V Alpines were among the first cars to have alternators and are negative earth. They were the Lucas 10AC type with a 4TR regulator, a 6RA relay and a 3AW warning light 'simulator.' The latter part is the least reliable, but there is a fix. Many Alpines now have later or modern alternators with a built-in regulator.

The original mechanical fuel pump is fine (though ethanol may eventually prove to be incompatible), but some owners prefer an electric pump. Ideally, this should have an accident cut-out switch.

The main loom passes along the left side of the car, along the edge of the floor and into the left rear wing. The main battery lead follows the same route but crosses to the box under the rear seat. Check the box for rust, that the battery is an appropriate size (close to filling the box), and that the terminals are clean and sound. The box lid should have brackets to hold the battery in place when closed.

Check all the wires under the bonnet for damage, embrittlement (near the exhaust) and poor routing and connections. Also, try to check wiring under the dashboard, and, of course, check that everything works …

Wheels and tyres

Alpines were supplied with either 4.5J x 13 steel wheels (with chrome hubcaps and rings) or 4J x 13 wire wheels. They are not immediately interchangeable as the hubs are different. The original tyres were 5.60 x 13 or 6.00 x 13 crossplies. The nearest radial equivalent would be 165/82 x 13, but most cars have 165/80 x 13. Many Alpines now have wider alloy wheels which will take wider, lower-profile tyres.

Many non-standard wheels need a thin spacer because the drum is dished slightly.

Check the make, condition, size and age of every tyre, including the spare. Tyres from 1990 onwards have a code. Three digits mean the tyres are pre-2000. From 2000 they have four digits, two for the week and two for the year: 3004 is July 2004. If more than ten years old, budget for early replacement.

If the car has non-standard wheels try to check the rears. The Alpine drums are dished. Some alloy wheels do not clear the dishing and require thin spacers. This is an important safety issue.

The engine compartment

Pull the bonnet release. Check that the bonnet opens readily and can then be lifted

The Series 3-V brake servo is mounted front-right. This is a Girling Mk2B, very similar on the outside to the original Mk2A except for the vacuum chamber clamp. Many Alpines now have a recent 'Lockheed type' servo, as the old Girlings are often beyond a rebuild.

(there's no additional safety catch to release). Does it close easily?

Check the chassis plate on the flat area next to the bonnet lock. It will give you the Series, its sequential number, the model (home, export, GT), the paint colour code and whether it had overdrive. Does it agree with the paper documentation (V5 in the UK)?

Check the engine number which faces upwards just in front of the oil filter. Originally, it will have been the same as the chassis number. Rootes replacement engines often had a plate on the left side, low down on the engine block, and no number in the usual place. An engine from another type will begin with a different code. Note that five-bearing engines (Series V) have their dipstick hole in the block casting. Earlier three-bearing motors have a tube on the side of the sump.

Check the breathing system of Series 3-V cars. There should be a pipe from the pushrod cover to a valve in the manifold. Later cars also have a flame-trap connected to the oil filler and to the air cleaner inlet. If the engine breathes 'overboard' from here onto the road, ask why. (Note that it is fine to run the new Weber conversion with a breather through a filter to atmosphere).

Ask if the cylinder head has been converted to run on unleaded fuel. There should be new exhaust valve seats and bronze valve guide liners. Ask to see an invoice for the work.

Take a general look at what you see. Is it neat and fairly clean? Any major fluid

Series V Alpines with the 1725 have twin Stromberg CD150 carburettors. They also have a Lucas 10AC alternator with 4TR regulator in place of the old dynamo and RB340 regulator.

The crossflow radiator of the Series I-II with its characteristic cast aluminium header tank. No brake servo (but a Clayton Dewandre was an option). Twin Zenith carburettors.

The 1725 engine, gearbox and overdrive. The overdrive requires a special gearbox mainshaft, and a shorter propshaft. Switches for reversing lights and the overdrive interlock are at the front of the remote assembly. The 1725's dipstick goes into a hole in the block casting just behind the oil filter, and the block has cast lugs with tapped holes later used for the Arrow engine mounts. (Courtesy Tim Raymond)

leaks? Any rust on components or the bodyshell? Any obvious modifications such as an electric fan, fuel filter or pump, non-standard servo, horns, carburettors? Any sign of front accident damage?

Cooling system 4 3 2 1

Series I-II have a crossflow radiator with a cast aluminium header tank in front of the cylinder head. Later cars have a conventional system. Check for leaks. Check the colour of the coolant. It should be blue – not pink (modern organic antifreeze which is incompatible with traditional antifreeze). Check that the heater is connected. The feed is on the cylinder head; the return is on the water pump.

Try to check the radiator matrix for leaks or damage. If the car has both a mechanical fan and an electric fan, ask why. Fitting an electric fan is a good idea, but the mechanical one should not then be needed. If it has an electric fan, is it operated manually or by a thermostatic switch?

Water dripping from the rear of the engine could be the core plug in front of the flywheel. Not a quick fault to fix.

Series V cars have a conventional radiator and a simple bag for screenwasher fluid.

Steering system 4 3 2 1

The Alpine steering system has a 'box' at the lower end of the column. The link to the nearside suspension passes over the bellhousing, so there are lots of joints. Check for wear; ask someone to gently move the wheel back and forth a few degrees while you look. The wheel itself should have only minimal free play. Check the swinging link below the box for free movement – try to move one end up and down. Check the outer trackrod ends for wear and for rubber boot damage.

Check the oil level by removing the plastic bung (it should be EP90 oil, not ordinary grease), and check the box for leaks at the bottom.

Brake and clutch hydraulics 4 3 2 1

Series 3-V Alpines were built with a Girling Mk2A vacuum servo; initially 5in diameter, then 7in later. Earlier cars could be fitted with a Clayton Dewandre servo as an option, but this is rare. Some Alpines have the later improved Mk2B servo, but many owners now choose the safer option of fitting a new Lockheed-type servo. Some are sold by Capari, the descendant of Lockheed; others are of Asian origin. The new servo can be fitted in the original location (engine bay front, right) but it must have secure mountings.

The Burman recirculating-ball steering box. Series 3-V cars have an adjustable steering column.

Original RHD Alpine Girling master cylinders had built-in cast aluminium reservoirs. Some replacements have plastic reservoirs. Callipers and wheel cylinders are Girling. The clutch hydraulics are conventional, but were made by Lockheed.

Rootes used cheap steel pipes which should by now have been replaced. Look for copper or, better still, 'cunifer' (copper-nickel alloy).

The brakelight switch is in the hydraulic system and 'pattern' replacements are often unsatisfactory. Check that the lights come on (ignition on) with light foot pressure.

Fuel system

4 3 2 1

Tanks and pipes will by now have been checked. The original fuel pump was an AC mechanical unit driven from the front of the camshaft. It had a glass bowl; later replacements often lack this. The pumps can be rebuilt. Early cars had metal pipes; later vehicles used nylon. Owners often replace pipes with rubber. It is vital that any replacement pipe material is not harmed by the ethanol in modern fuel. Unless the rubber pipe is recent, you cannot be certain.

The pipe from the pump to the carburettors originally passed just below the thermostat housing. Some owners find that modern fuels give rise to vaporising problems, and they change the pipe route. Check that the routing and clipping are secure, and that there is allowance for engine movement.

Original mechanical fuel pumps have glass tops. Many replacements have just steel covers. Some owners prefer an electric pump.

Front suspension and brakes

4 3 2 1

Series I-3 Alpines had greased metal wishbone and kingpin bushes. Series IV-V had rubber wishbone bushes and sealed outer ball joints. To check for wear you MUST jack the car under the outer end of the wishbone to remove load from the rebound stop under the upper wishbone. With the wheel off the ground, try to rock or lift each front wheel. You should detect minimal freedom in the taper-roller hub bearings but nothing else. The Series IV-V wishbone rubber bushes may *look* poor but are fine if there is no radial play. Check the bump stop on the lower wishbone and the rebound stop on top of the crossmember for damage to the rubber. Also check the boots fitted to later cars' ball joints.

Check the shock absorbers for leaks or damage to

Series I-3 cars have metal bushes for both wishbone pivots and the outer trunnion and kingpin.

their mounting bushes. Check what type they are. Spax are yellow and have adjusting screws. With the car on the ground, push down hard on each front corner and release. The car should then just rise and stop – no bounces.

The Series IV and V right front suspension. The wishbone inner pivots are rubber bushes; the outer pivots are spherical ball joints, as are all four trackrod ends. The shock absorbers are inside the coil springs. (Courtesy Tim Raymond)

The complete front crossmember and suspension. The two cast aluminium wedges set the castor angle, but they can corrode away. (Courtesy Goldsmith family)

Check that the car has a front anti-roll bar. All Alpines have them but occasionally, once removed, they are not refitted.

Check the condition of each brake disc, and check the hoses and callipers for leaks or damage.

Rear suspension, axle and brakes ④ ③ ② ①

Check the shock absorbers as above. Series I-II cars had lever-arm dampers; later cars have the telescopic type.

You should already have checked to see whether the car sits level. If it doesn't, you might ask to jack each end in turn, on the exact centre line (under the crossmember at the front; under the diff at the rear). If it goes level, the problem (eg a weak spring) is at the end you jacked.

The rear springs should be almost flat when the car is parked. With the car securely raised, check the springs for any broken leaves or obvious damage to the rubber bushes at their ends.

It's convenient at this time to also check for serious differential oil leaks or problems with the handbrake linkage. There is a breather cap at the top of the differential casing. You will find oil stains around it.

Unless you wish, and are allowed, to remove the wheels and drums, all you can check on the rear brakes is for any sign of oil leaks at the drum rim and on the backplate, the functioning of the handbrake, and the general condition of the flexible hose to the axle.

All Alpines should have an anti-roll bar attached to the lower wishbones by four clamps and rubber bushes. Some go missing during restoration.

The rear axle and suspension could hardly be simpler. Removal of the differential requires the halfshaft/hub/brake assemblies to be pulled out. (Courtesy Tim Raymond)

Ignition system ④ ③ ② ①

Check whether the original Lucas 25D distributor, with vacuum advance, has been modified or replaced. Kits which replace the mechanical points with a magnetic sensor can work very well, and are a good alternative if there are doubts about the quality of reproduction points and condensers.

Complete new electronic distributors are available (probably for less money than a properly rebuilt original). Check the coil age and type. New cheap coils tend to run hot and often have limited lives; a good original Lucas unit may be better. Check the HT leads for damage and fit. If copper cored, they should have suppressed sparkplug caps.

Engine oil system   ② ①

Pull the dipstick, preferably when the engine is cold. The oil should not only be at the correct level, but also be fairly clean, not thick and black. Ask when the oil and filter were last changed – it should be an annual task. Remove the oil filler cap and look for any sign of 'mayonnaise' in the rocker cover, a sign of possible cylinder head gasket failure.

Check the engine for serious leaks – expect some oil, but not a puddle after every stop. The front pulley has a scroll rather than a seal, but a modification kit is available.

Alpine Series V cars were built with an oil cooler in front of the radiator. At first, the pipes were routed down, forward and across the car by the radiator, but later cars have one pipe passing over the top of the engine. Check for pipe rubbing damage and perishing of the rubber hoses.

Starting

You should try to arrange to witness a cold start. Most cars, especially Series V, will need full choke to start, and some choke for a few miles. Expect the engine to turn rather slowly on the starter – it's small for its task, and the cable is long. Watch the oil pressure gauge. If the car has been standing for a week or more, it may take two or three seconds to register pressure, but then the pressure should rise quickly to 50psi or more. When hot, it may idle at only 25psi, but when above about 2000rpm, the three-bearing engines should show 50psi, and the SV should be at 40psi.

If you have any doubts about the cylinder head gasket, remove the radiator cap while still cold and look for bubbles while running.

The ammeter, if fitted, should show charge when the engine is speeded up.

Driving

Even if you plan to undertake a complete rebuild after purchase, it is good to know exactly what you have, so a thorough test drive is recommended. Make sure you are properly insured.

First impressions will depend on both the car and your own driving experience. The Alpine's steering will feel much heavier than any modern car, especially when manoeuvring slowly. Series I-II unservoed brakes will also be a shock. Conversely, compared to other cars from the 1960s, the later Alpines will feel quite modern, with pleasant controls (once moving), a very comfortable ride, and adequate to brisk performance. Only the steering may feel less precise than in today's cars.

The temperature should rise within two-three miles to 80-85°C and then stay there. If it varies a lot, the thermostat may be defective or missing – and if it's missing, you need to find out why. Once the engine is properly warm check the idle. It should be reasonably smooth, and at about 1000rpm.

Check each gear in drive and on the over-run – it should not jump out. Gears should engage easily, but you will need full clutch travel.

The car should maintain a straight course but respond well enough to steering inputs. Try accelerating in third to at least 60mph. Does the car respond well? At the other extreme, a well-sorted Alpine should be fine at 25mph in direct fourth gear.

Test the overdrive, if fitted. In fourth at about 40mph, move the OD switch down while keeping a light throttle applied. You should hear the engine speed drop almost immediately. Then apply *more* throttle and disengage OD. The revs will rise. The car may jerk a little and it's generally better to dip the clutch while disengaging overdrive. Overdrive should also work in third gear, but not first, second or reverse.

Try braking (check your mirror). Cars with a servo should slow and stop well – though remember there is no ABS or other electronic trickery. Locking all wheels should be possible. It is not uncommon for the brakes to 'pull' *slightly*. Alpines without a servo require much more effort, though they are effective. Also check the handbrake. A good one will just lock the rear wheels.

Now use your ears. Listen for 'clonks' from the driveline when applying or releasing the accelerator – propshaft U/Js, worn wire wheel splines or axle perhaps. Also for noise and vibrations coming from the exhaust touching the chassis. A vibration felt via the accelerator pedal at high revs may indicate that the inlet manifold is not tight on the head. A 'zizz' from the gearlever was a known irritant when the cars were new, and can be fixed with grease or a shim.

Try the car with the roof raised or the hardtop fitted. You can better assess some of the noises described here, and check on noise resulting from poor seals or window adjustment. You can check that the heater demists the screen and warms the car.

Speedometer and rev-counter

There are often issues with speedometer and/or rev-counter accuracy and now is the time to check.

The speedometer can be checked with a GPS app on a smartphone; alternatively, in the UK, use a stopwatch to measure the time taken to pass 16 of the 100m posts (= 1 mile) found alongside dual-carriageways. Expect the speedometer to read fast, partly through age, partly because Rootes erred that way, and partly because the tyres may be smaller than the originals.

Series I-IV cable-driven rev-counters may read a little high; the later electronic types in Series IV-V often read high to very high (they can be rebuilt and calibrated). At 50mph, the engine of a Series I, II, IV or V fitted with OD but *not* engaged should be about 3050rpm. All Series 3 Alpines, and any not built with OD should run at 2800rpm.

If your measurements don't agree, then something, somewhere, is wrong. It could be just the rev-counter, or it may be that the axle or speedo drive gears, the speedo itself, or the tyres are different.

At the end of your drive leave the engine running, open the bonnet, get out and listen to the engine. You may hear some valve noise. Be concerned if there is a noise which is only from one cylinder – a knock, tap, hiss, etc. Use the throttle linkage to rev up the engine while you listen and watch. Check for noises from the water pump or dynamo/alternator. At idle, remove the oil filler cap. There should not be a significant change in running, or big emissions of fumes.

Roadworthiness test certificate

MoT in the UK; TUV or DEKRA test in Germany; Control Technique in France and varied or no requirement in the USA – this and a valid 'Title' are important considerations if buying there. Ask to see the latest certification and check its date. Failure information is as useful as a pass certificate.

Evaluation procedure

Add up the total points scored: **136 points** = first class, possibly concours; **95 points** = good/very good; **70 points** = average; **35 points** = poor. A car scoring over 100 should be completely usable and require the minimum of repair, although continued maintenance and care will be required to keep it in condition. Cars scoring between 35 and 70 points will require a full restoration – the cost of which will be much the same regardless of the points scored. Cars scoring between 70 and 100 points will require very careful assessment of the necessary repair/restoration costs in order to decide a realistic purchase value.

10 Auctions
– sold! Another way to buy your dream

Auction pros & cons
Pros: Prices will usually be lower than those of dealers or private sellers and you might grab a real bargain on the day. Auctioneers have usually established clear title with the seller. At the venue you should be able to examine documentation relating to the vehicle.

Cons: You have to rely on a sketchy catalogue description of condition & history. The opportunity to inspect is limited and you cannot drive the car. Auction cars are often a little below par and may require some work. It's easy to overbid. There will usually be a buyer's premium to pay in addition to the auction hammer price.

Which auction?
Auctions by established auctioneers are advertised in car magazines and on the auction houses' websites. A catalogue, or a simple printed list of the lots for auctions might only be available a day or two ahead, though often lots are listed and pictured on auctioneers' websites much earlier. Contact the auction company to ask if previous auction selling prices are available as this is useful information (details of past sales are often available on websites).

Catalogue, entry fee and payment details
When you purchase the catalogue of the vehicles in the auction, it often acts as a ticket allowing two people to attend the viewing days and the auction. Catalogue details tend to be comparatively brief, but will include information such as 'one owner from new, low mileage, full service history,' etc. It will also usually show a guide price to give you some idea of what to expect to pay, and will tell you what is charged as a 'Buyer's premium.' The catalogue will also contain details of acceptable forms of payment. At the fall of the hammer an immediate deposit is usually required, the balance payable within 24 hours. If the plan is to pay by cash there may be a cash limit. Some auctions will accept payment by debit card. Sometimes credit or charge cards are acceptable, but will often incur an extra charge. A bank draft or bank transfer will have to be arranged in advance with your own bank as well as with the auction house. No car will be released before **all** payments are cleared. If delays occur in payment transfers then storage costs can accrue.

Buyer's premium
A buyer's premium will be added to the hammer price: **don't** forget this in your calculations. It is not usual for there to be a further state tax or local tax on the purchase price and/or on the buyer's premium.

Viewing
In some instances it's possible to view on the day, or days before, as well as in the hours prior to, the auction. There are auction officials available who are willing to help out by opening engine and luggage compartments and to allow you to inspect the interior. While the officials may start the engine for you, a test drive is out of the

question. Crawling under and around the car as much as you want is permitted, but you can't suggest that the car you are interested in be jacked up, or attempt to do the job yourself. You can also ask to see any documentation available.

Bidding

Before you take part in the auction, **decide your maximum bid – and stick to it!**

It may take a while for the auctioneer to reach the lot you are interested in, so use that time to observe how other bidders behave. When it's the turn of your car, attract the auctioneer's attention and make an early bid. The auctioneer will then look to you for a reaction every time another bid is made, usually the bids will be in fixed increments until the bidding slows, when smaller increments will often be accepted before the hammer falls. If you want to withdraw from the bidding, make sure the auctioneer understands your intentions – a vigorous shake of the head when he or she looks to you for the next bid should do the trick!

Assuming that you are the successful bidder, the auctioneer will note your card or paddle number, and from that moment on you will be responsible for the vehicle. If the car is unsold, either because it failed to reach the reserve or because there was little interest, it may be possible to negotiate with the owner, via the auctioneers, after the sale is over.

Successful bid

There are two more items to think about. How to get the car home, and insurance. If you can't drive the car, your own or a hired trailer is one way, another is to have the vehicle shipped using the facilities of a local company. The auction house will also have details of companies specialising in the transfer of cars.

Insurance for immediate cover can usually be purchased on site, but it may be more cost-effective to make arrangements with your own insurance company in advance, and then call to confirm the full details.

eBay & other online auctions?

eBay & other online auctions could land you a car at a bargain price, though you'd be foolhardy to bid without examining the car first, something most vendors encourage. A useful feature of eBay is that the geographical location of the car is shown, so you can narrow your choices to those within a realistic radius of home. Be prepared to be outbid in the last few moments of the auction. Remember, your bid is binding and that it will be very, very difficult to get restitution in the case of a crooked vendor fleecing you – *caveat emptor!*

Be aware that some cars offered for sale in online auctions are 'ghost' cars. **Don't** part with **any** cash without being sure that the vehicle does actually exist and is as described (usually pre-bidding inspection is possible).

Auctioneers

Barrett-Jackson www.barrett-jackson.com
Bonhams www.bonhams.com
British Car Auctions (BCA) www.bca-europe.com
or www.british-car-auctions.co.uk
Cheffins www.cheffins.co.uk

Christies www.christies.com
Coys www.coys.co.uk
eBay www.ebay.com
H&H www.classic-auctions.co.uk
RM www.rmauctions.com
Shannons www.shannons.com.au
Silver www.silverauctions.com

11 Paperwork
– correct documentation is essential!

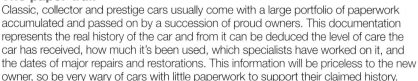

The paper trail
Classic, collector and prestige cars usually come with a large portfolio of paperwork accumulated and passed on by a succession of proud owners. This documentation represents the real history of the car and from it can be deduced the level of care the car has received, how much it's been used, which specialists have worked on it, and the dates of major repairs and restorations. This information will be priceless to the new owner, so be very wary of cars with little paperwork to support their claimed history.

Registration documents
All countries/states have some form of registration for private vehicles, whether it's the American 'pink slip' system or the British 'log book' system.

It is essential to check that the registration document is genuine, that it relates to the car in question, and that all the vehicle's details are correctly recorded, including chassis/VIN and engine numbers (if these are shown). The previous owner's name and address will be recorded in the document, unless you are buying from a dealer.

In the UK the current (Euro-aligned) registration document is named 'V5C,' and is printed in coloured sections of red, blue, green and yellow. The blue section relates to the car specification, the green section has details of the new owner and is sent to the DVLA in the UK when the car is sold. A small section in yellow deals with selling the car within the motor trade. In the UK the DVLA will provide details of earlier keepers of the vehicle upon payment of a small fee, and much can be learned in this way.

If the car has a foreign registration there may be expensive and time-consuming formalities to complete. The difficulty is increased enormously if relevant paperwork from the previous country is not available.

Roadworthiness certificate
Most country/state administrations require that vehicles are regularly tested to prove they are safe to use on the public highway and do not produce excessive emissions. In the UK that test (the MoT) is carried out at approved testing stations, for a fee. In the USA the requirement varies, but most states insist on an emissions test every two years as a minimum, while the police are charged with pulling over unsafe-looking vehicles.

In the UK the test is required annually, but pre-1960 cars are now exempt. As certificates show the mileage reading, they form an independent record of that car's history. Ask the seller if previous certificates are available. Without an MoT the vehicle should be trailered to its new home, unless you insist that a valid MoT is part of the deal. (Not such a bad idea this, as at least you will know the car was roadworthy on the day it was tested.You don't need to wait for the old certificate to expire before having the test done.)

Road licence
The administration of every country/state requires some form of road licence. How it is displayed varies enormously from country to country and state to state.

Whatever the form of the road licence, it must relate to the vehicle carrying it and be present and valid if the car is to be driven on the public highway legally. The value of the licence will depend on the length of time it will continue to be valid. Changed legislation in the UK means that the seller of a car must surrender any existing road fund licence, and it is the responsibility of the new owner to re-tax the vehicle at the time of purchase and before the car can be driven on the road. It's therefore vital to see the Vehicle Registration Certificate (V5C) at the time of purchase, and to have access to the New Keeper Supplement (V5C/2), allowing the buyer to obtain road tax immediately. In the UK, vehicles built more than 40 years ago (all Alpines) are licenced free of charge, but there is still an annual renewal with the DVLA. If a car is not licenced for road use it must have a SORN (Statutory Off-Road Notification).

Certificates of authenticity

A certificate (Heritage Certificate) proving the age and authenticity of a particular vehicle may be available, so if the car has one of these it is a definite bonus. If you want to obtain one, the relevant owners' club is the best starting point.

If the car has been used in European classic car rallies it may have a FIVA (Fédération Internationale des Véhicules Anciens) certificate, which enables organisers and participants to see if a particular vehicle is suitable for individual events. If you want to obtain such a certificate see www.fbhvc.co.uk or www.fiva.org. There will be similar organisations in other countries too.

Valuation certificate

Hopefully, the vendor will have a recent valuation certificate, or letter signed by a recognised expert stating how much that particular car is deemed to be worth (such documents, together with photos, are usually needed to get 'agreed value' insurance). Generally such documents should act only as confirmation of your own assessment of the car, rather than a guarantee of value, as the expert may not have seen the car in the flesh. The easiest way to find out how to obtain a formal valuation is to contact the owners' club.

Service history

Often these cars will have been serviced at home by enthusiastic (and hopefully capable) owners for many years. Try to obtain as much service history and other paperwork pertaining to the car as you can. Specialist garage receipts score most points in the value stakes. However, anything helps in the great authenticity game, items like the original bill of sale, handbook, parts invoices and repair bills add to the story and character of the car. A brochure correct to the year of the car's manufacture is valuable. If the seller claims that the car has been restored, then expect receipts and other evidence from a specialist restorer. If the seller claims to have carried out regular servicing, ask what work was completed, when, and seek some evidence. Your assessment of the car's overall condition should tell you whether the seller's claims are genuine.

Restoration photographs

If the seller tells you that the car has been restored, then expect to be shown a series of photographs taken while the restoration was under way. Pictures taken at various stages, and from various angles, should help you gauge the thoroughness of the work. If you buy the car, ask if you can have all the photographs as they form an important part of the vehicle's history. It's surprising how many sellers are happy to part with their car and accept your cash, but want to hang on to their photographs! In the latter event, you may be able to persuade the vendor to get a set of copies made.

12 What's it worth?
– let your head rule your heart

Condition
If the car you've been looking at is really bad, then you've probably not bothered to use the marking system in Chapter 9, 60 minute evaluation. You may not have even got as far as using that chapter at all!

If you did use the marking system in Chapter 9 you'll know whether the car is in Excellent (maybe Concours), Good, Average or Poor condition or, perhaps, somewhere in-between these categories.

Many classic/collector car magazines run a regular price guide. If you haven't bought the latest editions, do so now and compare their suggested values for the model you are thinking of buying: also look at the auction prices they're reporting. Values of good examples of most classic cars have risen since savings interest rates have been very low, but some models will always be more sought-after than others. Trends can change too. The values published in the magazines tend to vary from one magazine to another, as do their scales of condition, so read carefully the guidance notes they provide. Bear in mind that a car that is truly a recent show winner could be worth more than the highest scale published. Assuming that the car you have in mind is not in show/concours condition, then relate the level of condition that you judge the car to be in with the appropriate guide price. How does the figure compare with the asking price? Before you start haggling with the seller, consider what affect any variation from standard specification might have on the car's value.

If you are buying from a dealer, remember there will be a dealer's premium on the price.

Desirable options/extras
Overdrive is highly desirable as it gives you six forward gears and more relaxed motorway cruising.

Wheels are subject to personal taste, but good wire wheels (with unworn mounting splines) or attractive alloy wheels (especially if they are a little wider than the factory 4.5J wheels) are desirable. 14in (in place of 13in) wheels allow the use of lower profile tyres.

A cylinder head properly modified with new exhaust valve seats and bronze guide inserts is desirable (the conversion costs about ●x250 excluding fitting).

A hardtop makes the car snug and quieter in winter, but some buyers don't want one because they only intend the car for summer use, and the top has to be stored somewhere.

Definitely worth more with overdrive. The overdrive cannot be easily fitted to an ordinary gearbox as a different mainshaft is required. The propshaft is also shorter. (Courtesy Tim Raymond)

Some like wire wheels and are prepared to pay. But they do require periodic checks and re-alignment, and splines wear if the mounting nuts are not very tight. (Courtesy Goldsmith family)

GTs are worth less as there is no alternative weather protection if you leave the stylish hardtop at home.
(Courtesy Tim Raymond)

GTs were supplied with these removable sun visors. Hard to find if they are missing.

An electric fan (*replacing* the engine-driven fan) reduces noise and wear, speeds warm-up, and provides cooling when needed.

A period radio in the original optional console below the dashboard is desirable, but for listening pleasure you will need an FM conversion.

Undesirable features

It is not only *what* has been done but *how well* it has been done that matters. However, an iron-head Rootes engine is definitely undesirable, and a non-Rootes

The accessory radio and speaker console is nice to have. The original aluminium trim has been replaced by wood veneer, and extra switches have been added to the author's car here.

engine (Toyota V6, Ford Zetec) or body modifications such as bulged wheelarches or wild paint schemes/colours have very limited appeal.

Striking a deal

Negotiate on the basis of your condition assessment, the history/ownership record, mileage, and fault rectification cost. Also take into account the car's specification. Be realistic about the value, but don't be completely intractable: a small compromise on the part of the vendor or buyer will often facilitate a deal at little real cost.

www.velocebooks.com / www.veloce.co.uk
All current books • New book news • Special offers • Gift vouchers

13 Do you really want to restore?

– it'll take longer and cost more than you think

The real questions are, how much restoration are you willing to take on, and who is going to do it? Some people are quite happy to do major mechanical work but not bodywork, trim or, more often, electrical work. The usual advice – 'buy the best you can afford' – applies here. The difficulty lies in judging which is the best, and whether it is as good as it may seem. This book should help you to minimise later disappointment.

Alpines can still be found in rough condition in barns. You might think that being stored away for many years means that a car will be basically good, but this is rarely the case. Many Alpines used throughout the year in their early life were very, very rusty in less than ten years. The car's structure is very complicated; it has lots of parts and panels.

These alarming photographs of the remains of the right side sill were taken as Dave Holcombe began restoration of his red Series II in 1980, when the car was only 18 years old.
(Courtesy Dave Holcombe)

A further problem is that cars left unused tend to be relieved of rare parts. Before you even think about taking on a basket case, especially if it is an early Series I or II Alpine, be absolutely sure that it is complete. It must have not only all its mechanical assemblies, but also all the small fittings and trim pieces.
Then think about a complete structural restoration. If you have the space, time, skills, equipment and enthusiasm, to do it may be worthwhile. If you have to pay someone, you will be better off buying a good car in the first place. Reproduction panels and part-panels are available, but they are largely hand-made and expensive. A badly rusted shell will have to be mounted in some sort of jig to maintain its shape while being repaired. A roll-over frame may be a good investment.

A rust-free Alpine from Arizona, or similar, with sun-dried rubber, paint and trim is usually a much better bet, even if the car is poor mechanically, and is LHD.

Any car which has been around for five decades will be fortunate if it has not, at some time, received attention from someone whose standard of work, and probably financial resources, too, were less than desirable. Cars that have suffered badly tend to be sold on quickly as new owners discover older DIY horrors.

If you cannot do major

It required time and skill (and hence money) but Dave's Series II (pictured throughout this book) was successfully restored.
(Courtesy Dave Holcombe)

metal and paintwork yourself, there is great scope for assembling all the body, trim, fittings and electrics, as these are time-consuming and therefore expensive to have completed professionally. Nothing here is particularly difficult; it just needs care, time, a logical approach – and a degree of agility and dexterity. There is one other requirement; space. A car in pieces occupies about three times as much area as a complete vehicle. And parts need to be labelled, bagged or boxed, and then stored carefully. The space must be under cover. You cannot undertake a restoration on the front drive.

Allocating a 'difficulty of restoration' score may help put all this into context. If a Rolls-Royce Silver Shadow scores 10, an E Type Jaguar scores 9, and the Morris Minor and the MGB are at about 3, then an Alpine is around 5 or 6.

The bodyshell

Rootes had three aims when the car was designed. The first was to make the Alpine look good. The second was to use as much as possible from other vehicles in its range, and the third was to make the shell really stiff. It started with the Husky (a shortened estate version of the Minx). This had the correct wheelbase (7ft 2in), and its underframe had all the necessary mountings for suspension, gearbox, etc. Rootes knew that an open car would need stiffening so it added three deep sill sections. These proved to be inadequate, so box sections in a large X form were added below the floor. Finally, it found that struts from the front wheelarches to the bulkhead were needed. The existing frame and mechanical parts dictated the space envelope and dimensions for the body. It works, but it's complicated.

Mechanical systems

These are mostly straightforward and robust. Many parts are common to contemporary Rootes saloons, but there are often detail changes. Spring dimensions, steering geometry, gear ratios and brakes are different. Few special tools are needed – the correct puller for the rear hubs and some simple tools for gearbox overhaul.

Trim and fittings

These take time: doors in particular are complex; there are about 14 possible adjustments to doors and winding windows. As it's a 1960s car, there are lots of chrome parts, and replating is not only expensive, but platers' quality varies. You will also need time to find missing trim parts, especially for an early Alpine.

Help and advice

Rootes' own workshop manuals are excellent for mechanical systems. Other useful books and online forums are listed in Chapter 16.

A restored shell after an acid dip and electrolytic priming. (Courtesy Tim Raymond)

New repair panels ready to fit to Tom Goldsmith's Series 3. The joins were originally hidden by lead loading. (Courtesy Goldsmith family)

14 Paint problems

– bad complexion, including dimples, pimples and bubbles

Paint faults generally occur due lack of protection/maintenance, or to poor preparation prior to a respray or touch-up. Some of the following conditions may be present in the car you're looking at:

Orange peel
This appears as an uneven paint surface, similar to the appearance of the skin of an orange. The fault is caused by the failure of atomised paint droplets to flow into each other when they hit the surface. It's sometimes possible to rub out the effect with proprietary paint, cutting/rubbing compound, or very fine grades of abrasive paper. A respray may be necessary in severe cases. Consult a bodywork repairer/paint shop for advice on the particular car.

Cracking
Severe cases are likely to have been caused by too heavy an application of paint (or filler beneath the paint). Also, insufficient stirring of the paint before application can lead to the components being improperly mixed, and cracking can result. Incompatibility with the paint already on the panel can have a similar effect. To rectify the problem it is necessary to rub down to a smooth, sound finish before respraying the problem area.

Crazing
Sometimes the paint takes on a crazed rather than a cracked appearance when the problems mentioned under 'Cracking' are present. This problem can also be caused by a reaction between the underlying surface and the paint. Paint removal and respraying the problem area is usually the only solution.

Blistering
Almost always caused by corrosion of the metal beneath the paint. Usually perforation will be found in the metal and the damage will usually be worse than that suggested by the area of blistering. The metal will have to be repaired before repainting.

Micro blistering
Usually the result of an economy respray

Good panel fits, no ripples, and a good paint finish on this fully-restored Series 3. (Courtesy Goldsmith family)

where inadequate heating has allowed moisture to settle on the car before spraying. Consult a paint specialist, but usually damaged paint will have to be removed before partial or full respraying. Can also be caused by car covers that don't 'breathe.'

Fading
Some colours, especially reds, are prone to fading if subjected to strong sunlight for long periods without the benefit of polish protection. Sometimes proprietary paint restorers, and/or paint cutting/rubbing compounds will retrieve the situation. Often a respray is the only real solution.

Peeling
Often a problem with metallic paintwork when the sealing lacquer becomes damaged and begins to peel off. Poorly applied paint may also peel. The remedy is to strip and start again!

Dimples
Dimples in the paintwork are caused by the residue of polish (particularly silicone types) not being removed properly before respraying. Paint removal and repainting is the only solution.

Dents
Small dents are usually easily cured by the 'Dentmaster,' or equivalent process, that sucks or pushes out the dent (as long as the paint surface is still intact). Companies offering dent removal services usually come to your home: consult your telephone directory.

15 Problems due to lack of use
– just like their owners, Alpines need exercise!

Cars, like humans, are at their most efficient if they exercise regularly. A run of at least ten miles, once a week, is recommended for classics.

Seized components
Pistons in calipers, slave and master cylinders can seize. The clutch may seize if the plate becomes stuck to the flywheel due to corrosion. Handbrakes (parking brakes) can seize if the cables and linkages rust. Pistons can seize in the bores due to corrosion.

Fluids
Old acidic oil can corrode bearings. Uninhibited coolant WILL corrode internal waterways, especially in the aluminium cylinder head. Lack of antifreeze can also cause core plugs to be pushed out, and even cracks in the block or head. Silt settling and solidifying will cause overheating. Brake fluid absorbs water from the atmosphere and should be renewed every two years (unless silicone fluid is used). Old fluid with a high water content will cause corrosion and perhaps brake failure when the water turns to vapour near hot braking components. Pistons/calipers often seize (freeze).

Tyre problems
Tyres that have had the weight of the car on them in a single position for some time will develop flat spots, resulting in some (usually temporary) vibration. The tyre walls may have cracks or (blister-type) bulges, meaning new tyres are needed. Check date codes.

Shock absorbers (dampers)
With lack of use, the dampers will lose their elasticity or even seize. Creaking, groaning and stiff suspension are signs of this problem.

Rubber and plastic
Radiator hoses may have perished and split, possibly resulting in the loss of all coolant. Window and door seals can harden and leak. Gaiters/boots can crack. Wiper blades will harden.

Electrics
The battery will be of little use if it has not been kept charged. Earthing/grounding problems are common when the connections have corroded. This particularly applies to the Alpine's simple Lucas two-fuse box. Old bullet- and spade-type electrical connectors commonly rust/corrode and will need disconnecting, cleaning and protection (eg: Vaseline). Sparkplug electrodes may have corroded in an unused engine. Wiring insulation can harden and fail, especially near the exhaust.

Rotting exhaust system
Exhaust gas contains a high water content so exhaust systems corrode very quickly from the inside when the car is not used.

Shiny and new front brake – but if the car isn't used, the discs will rust and the calliper pistons will seize. (Courtesy Goldsmith family)

16 The Community
– key people, organisations and companies in the Alpine world

Clubs

UK
- Sunbeam Alpine Owners Club: www.saoc.demon.co.uk/
The UK club, founded in 1977, with 800 members. The SAOC is part of the ARCC (see below), and is closely associated with the Rootes Archive Centre Trust: http://www.rootesarchivecentre.org.uk/
- The Association of Rootes Car Clubs (the 'umbrella' organisation for UK Rootes clubs): http://www.thearcc.co.uk/

North America
- Sunbeam Alpine Owners Club of America: www.sunbeamalpine.org/
- Tigers East/Alpines East (TE/AE):
Tigers East/Alpines East, 7807 Charlotte Dr, Huntsville, AL 35802-2805
http://teae.org/
- Sunbeam Sportscar Owners Club of Canada (SSOCC):
PO BOX 483, Willowdale 'A,' Ontario, Canada, M2N 5T1

Europe
- Autoclub Grupo Rootes Espania
www.gruporootes.org
- Classic Sunbeam & Rootes de France
http://classicsunbeam.free.fr/
- Sunbeam Club de France
http://sunbeamclubfrance.free.fr/
- Rootes Club of Belgium
http://www.rootesclub.be/
- Rootes Denmark
http://www.rootes.dk/

- Rootes Club Nederland
http://www.rootesclub.nl/
- Rootes Car Club Norway
http://www.rootes.no/
- Rootes Car Club Sweden
http://www.rootes.se/
- Sunbeam Club Deutschland (SCD)
http://sunbeamclub.de.to
- Sunbeam Alpine Club Schweiz
http://www.sunbeamalpineclub.ch/

Alpines return to the city of their birth.

Almost 100 cars gather at the UK Sunbeam Alpine Owners' Club's annual 'National Meeting.'

Rest of the world
- Sunbeam Owners Club of New Zealand (SOC NZ). http://www.sunbeamcarclubofnewzealand.org.nz/
- Sunbeam Car Owners Club of South Australia
PO Box 112, Glenside SA 5065. http://www.sunbeamcarclubsa.org.au/
- The Sunbeam Owners' Club of NSW
PO Box 370, Epping NSW 1710
http://home.exetel.com.au/socnsw/

- Sunbeam Owners Club of Queensland Inc: PO Box 31, Underwood 4119, Queensland, Australia
www.qld.sunbeam.org.au/
- Sunbeam Car Club of Victoria Inc
PO Box 1, Lower Plenty, Victoria, Australia, 3093
www.sunbeamcarclubvictoria.com.au/content.asp?contentID=6
- Sunbeam Sports Car Club of S. Africa
http://www.sunbeamclub.co.za/

Technical and other forums
- Sunbeam Alpine Owners Club: http://alpine.forumup.com/ (See 'Alpine Technical Problems/Help' on main menu for the extensive technical forum.)
- Sunbeam Alpine Owners Club of America: http://www.sunbeamalpine.org/forum/

Parts suppliers
UK
- Alpine Innovations: 201 Hendon Way, London NW2 1JJ (+44) 2030 314882
- Alpine West Midlands Ltd: Units 7 & 8, r/o 271 Birchfield Rd, Headless Cross, Redditch, Worcs. B97 4NB (+44) 1527 401498 http://www.sunbeam-alpine.co.uk/
- BSAC: J L Hayter, 1 Carrington View, Tongue End, Spalding, PE11 3HZ (+44) 1775 670188
- Sunbeam Classic Spares: Chris Draycott, The Old Surgery, 8 Grimesgate, Diseworth, Derbyshire. DE74 2QD (+44) 1332 850856
- Sunbeam Spares Company Ltd: (+44) 1207 581025, www.thesunbeamsparescompany.co.uk/
- Speedy Spares: (+44) 1273 417889 or 412764 http://www.speedyspares.co.uk/
- Sunbeam Supreme: (+44) 116 2 742525, http://www.sunbeamsupreme.co.uk/

Non-UK
- Sunbeam Specialties Inc: 765 E McGlincy Lane Ste A, Campbell, CA 95008 Phone 408.371.1642, Fax 408.371.8070, http://www.rootes.com/index.html
- Rootes Post Vintage Spares (Netherlands): http://www.rootesparts.com/

Useful books
The Sunbeam Workshop Manual, Rootes WSM 124 (Factory manual for Alpine Series I-IV)
Rootes 'Light Car Range' Manual, WSM 145 (Factory manual for Alpine Series V)
The Alpine Guide. A compilation of technical articles, service bulletins and other information not found in the Rootes workshop manuals. Published by the SAOC.
Sunbeam Alpine Series I to V Parts List (Rootes official publication)
Alpine, The Classic Sunbeam by Chris McGovern. Gentry Books 1980
Sunbeam Alpine and Tiger by Graham Robson. Crowood Auto Classic 1996
The History of the Sunbeam Alpine by John Willshere. Amberley Books 2015

Rootes manuals and the parts list can often be found on eBay, sometimes in CD format.

17 Vital statistics
– essential data at your fingertips

Alpine production

Series	Production dates	Chassis prefix	CKD*	Number made	Engine cc
I	June 59-Sept 60	B900..	B909..	11,904	1494
II	Sept 60-Feb 63	B910..	B915..	19,956	1592
3	Jan 63-Oct 63	B920..	B925..	5863	1592
IV	Nov 63-Jul 64	B940..	B945..	7936	1592
IVa**	Aug 64-Aug 65	B941..	B946..	4470	1592
V	Aug 65-Jan 68	B395..	B3959..	19,122	1725

*Completely Knocked Down – supplied as partially-assembled kits for some export territories.

**Rootes never used the term 'Series IVa' but it is a convenient label to mark the introduction of significant changes.

Features by series
(This book follows Rootes' own practice of using Roman numerals for all Alpine series except for Series 3)

	I	II	3	IV	IVa	V
Fins	High	High	High	Low	Low	Low
Fuel Tanks/Boot	1/Small	1/Small	2/Large	2/Large	2/Large	2/Large
Carburettors	2 Zenith	2 Zenith	2Z or Solex	Solex	Solex	2 CD150
Roof shape	Rounded	Rounded	Angular	Angular	Angular	Angular
Models	Tourer	Tourer	Tourer, GT	Tourer, GT	Tourer, GT	Tourer, GT
Synchromesh	2,3,4	2,3,4	2,3,4	2,3,4	All	All
Fr suspension bushes	Metal	Metal	Metal	Rubber	Rubber	Rubber

Series V cars also have an alternator, footwell vents, twin reversing lights and an oil cooler.

Colour codes

1	**Embassy Black** – Known as jet black on brochures. (Series I-V)
8	**Foam Grey or Foam White –** Used on steel wheels SII-V. SI wheels were body-colour
11	**Thistle Grey** – A pale grey (Series I)
19	**Moonstone** – An extremely light grey, almost white. (Series I-IV)
30	**Seacrest Green** – A pale turquoise or eau-de-nil. Rootes racing livery. (Series II and prototypes)
39	**Carnival Red** – A very striking red with a hint of orange. (Series I-V except very late Series V)
40	**Glen Green** – A smoky mid green. (Series I)
52	**Lake Blue** – A mid blue. (Series II)
53	**Wedgwood Blue** – The light blue used on Wedgwood pottery. (Series II – IV)
58	**Midnight Blue** – A very dark and slightly greyish blue. (Late Series IV to early Series V)
61	**Quartz Blue Metallic** – A pale silver-blue (Series 3)
67	**Light Green Metallic** – Exactly as described. (Series 3)
68	**Autumn Gold Metallic** – A toned-down gold (Series 3)
76	**Balmoral Grey** – A mid grey. (Series IV and IVa)

86	**Forest Green** – Rootes' name for British Racing Green. (Late Series IV-late Series V)
92	**Arctic White** – Pure white but not quite the decorators' Brilliant White. (Series IV and V)
100	**Mediterranean Blue** – A light blue, but darker than Wedgwood Blue. (Series IVa and V)
102	**Oxford Blue** – A pure deep blue. (Late Series V)
106	**Commodore Blue** – A deep blue with just a hint of purple. (Late Series V)
107	**Holly Green** – A deep pure green, not as smoky as Forest Green. (Very late Series V)
108	**Polar White** – Off white, slightly creamier than Arctic White. (Late Series V)
109	**Orchid Green** – A vivid light green. (Late Series V)
122	**Signal Red** – A pure red, slightly darker and less orange than Carnival Red. (Very late Series V)
127	**Turquoise Blue Metallic** – A dark metallic turquoise. (Late Series V)
130	**Gunmetal Metallic** – A dark metallic grey. (Late Series V)

Engine data

Series	Capacity (cc, cu in)	Bore (in)	Stroke (in)	BHP (gross)	@rpm	Torque (lb/ft)
I	1494, 91.2	3.11	3.0	83.5	5300	89.5
II	1592, 97.1	3.21	3.0	85.5	5000	94
3 Tourer	1592, 97.1	3.21	3.0	87.7	5200	93
3 GT	1592, 97.1	3.21	3.0	80.2	5000	92
IV	1592, 97.1	3.21	3.0	86.1	5000	93.4
V	1725, 105.1	3.21	3.25	96.8	5400	103

GT versus Tourer – Series 3 to Series V

	Tourer	GT
Roof	Built-in soft top. Black steel hardtop available at extra cost.	Body coloured detachable hardtop only. Slightly more rear room as no hood stowage. Removable sun visors. Interior light.
Floor mats	Black rubber (carpet on gearbox tunnel)	Carpets
Dashboard	Black vinyl covering	Wood veneer
Steering wheel rim	Black plastic	Wood
Door trims	Plain. No cappings. Visible painted metal around the edges.	Trim covers whole door and has a welded pattern. Door capping (and matching quarterlight casting).

Panel corners and seams
Rounded door, boot and bonnet corners and lead loading to cover all panel joins were progressively deleted to save money, but changes did not always occur at a new 'Series.' Here is a summary:
• Series 3 onwards have square door lower front corners, and a visible join between sill and wing below.
• From approximately B941003065 (ie later Series IVa), the bonnet corners became square and a new visible joint was introduced, running aft from these corners to the screen. The door rear corners also became square, with a visible join between sill and rear wing below.
• From early in series V (B39500692), the boot rear corners became square.

THE ESSENTIAL MANUAL™

Classic British Car
Electrical
Systems

YOUR in-depth colour-illustrated guide
to understanding, repairing & improving
the electrical systems & components of
British classics

Rick Astley

Electrical systems used in British cars in the period 1950 to 1980
have gained some notoriety, most of it unfavourable and much of
it undeserved. This book shines a light on the subject, system by
system, including the murkier corners.

ISBN: 978-1-845849-48-1
Paperback • 27x20.7cm • £40* UK/$70* USA/$91 CAN
• 192 pages • 419 pictures
* prices subject to change, p&p extra

For more info on Veloce titles, visit our website at
www.veloce.co.uk • email: info@veloce.co.uk
• Tel: +44(0)1305 260068

Index